Gold EXPERIENCE

B1

Preliminary for Schools

Vocabulary and Grammar Workbook

Jill Florent
Suzanne Gaynor

Contents

 **24/7 teens**

VOCABULARY

1 Find twelve adjectives.

c	a	l	t	c	a	l	m	r
o	l	a	z	y	l	i	v	l
n	v	e	c	l	e	v	e	r
f	b	o	s	s	y	e	x	u
i	t	f	u	b	o	l	s	d
d	a	f	u	n	n	y	s	e
e	s	e	r	i	o	u	s	s
n	s	p	o	r	t	y	h	h
t	n	o	i	s	y	p	y	h

2 Match these words with the people in the pictures.

> calm   clever   lazy   ~~noisy~~   shy   sporty

1 ___noisy___   **2** _____

3 _____   **4** _____

5 _____   **6** _____

3 Complete the sentences with the correct adjectives. The first letter has been given.

1 Amelia works hard and she's feeling c_o_n_f_i_d_e_n_t about her exams.

2 Dylan tells everyone what to do, he's b_____ .

3 Charlie is r_____. He doesn't say please and thank you.

4 Grace makes us laugh. She's f_____ .

5 Ethan doesn't joke or laugh. He's s_____ .

6 Sophie always goes out and does lots of things. She's l_____ .

4 **GOLD EXPERIENCE**

4 **Write the words under the correct headings.**

| ~~bossy~~ calm clever confident |
| funny lazy lively noisy rude |

Positive	Negative
	bossy

5 **Choose the correct prepositions.**

1 We're excited *with/about/of* going to Rome.
2 Andy always wins. He's brilliant *at/of/with* playing tennis.
3 Don't worry, it's only a film. There's nothing to be frightened *with/at/of*.
4 We don't want Tony in the band. He's terrible *about/with/at* playing the guitar.
5 I'm really bored *at/with/in* watching TV. I want to go out.
6 John isn't interested *in/about/at* science. He wants to study history.

6 **Complete the sentences. Use one or two words in each space.**

1 James is ___*brilliant*___ at scoring goals.
2 We are _____ with doing boring things.
3 The children are _____ of the dark.
4 The students in my class are _____ about the school trip.
5 Chloe and Dan are _____ in geography.
6 Max is _____ at cooking. We can't eat the food he cooks.

7 **Match the adjectives (1–6) with the prepositions (a–f).**

1 brilliant   a with
2 excited   b about
3 terrible   c of
4 fed up   d in
5 frightened   e at
6 interested   f at

8 **Read the conversation and choose the best answer, A, B, C or D, for each space.**

Pat: Let's watch the rugby match between New Zealand and Australia.

Chris: You watch it. I'm not interested 1) _____ rugby.

Pat: Aren't you? I'm really excited 2) _____ it. New Zealand are brilliant 3) _____ rugby and I like the Haka, the 4) _____ dance they do before the match.

Chris: Are they doing the Haka now? Look! They're sticking out their tongues.

Pat: Yes, but they aren't being 5) _____.

Chris: And they aren't laughing, they're very 6) _____. Do you think the Australian team are 7) _____ of them?

Pat: No, I don't. The Australians are very good 8) _____ rugby.

Chris: My cousin is Australian. He's very 9) _____, he plays cricket and he loves surfing and swimming, too.

1 A about   (B) in
  C by   D with
2 A at   B of
  C about   D in
3 A at   B in
  C about   D by
4 A sporty   B lively
  C bossy   D calm
5 A confident   B funny
  C lazy   D rude
6 A funny   B clever
  C serious   D confident
7 A interested   B bored
  C excited   D frightened
8 A in   B by
  C at   D with
9 A confident   B sporty
  C funny   D shy

GRAMMAR

Present simple and present continuous

1 Write sentences and questions. Use the present simple.

1 Where / you / come / from / ?
   Where do you come from?

2 Jacob / not / work in a shop

3 They / not / play football every week

4 Lily / like / ice cream

5 They / eat / rice every day / ?

6 Ethan / know / a lot of people here

7 Jacob / be / good at playing tennis / ?

8 All my friends / be / interested in music

2 Complete the sentences with the present continuous form of the verbs in brackets.

1 *Is Jo coming* (Jo / come) to the party with us?

2 Excuse me, you _____ (sit) in my seat.

3 What _____ (you / try) to say?

4 What _____ (you / do) now?

5 I _____ (go) shopping in town this afternoon. I need some new shoes.

6 It _____ (freeze) today.

7 The sun _____ (not shine) at the moment.

8 Tom _____ (not skate) on the lake.

3 Choose the correct words.

1 What *are you doing*/do you do at the moment?

2 *I'm playing/I play* a computer game.

3 *Is it snowing*/Does it snow in the winter in your country?

4 It often *rains/is raining* in tropical countries.

5 *I'm not understanding/I don't understand* what you mean.

6 *He's coming/He comes* from Russia.

7 *We're learning/We learn* how to skate.

8 *She's wanting/She wants* to stay at home.

9 They *don't study/aren't studying* English this year.

10 *Does the sun shine/Is the sun shining* now?

4 Complete the sentences with the correct form of the verbs in brackets.

1 Where *does Aydin come* (Aydin / come) from?

2 Makana _____ (love) living near the sea.

3 Millions of tourists _____ (visit) Hawaii every year.

4 We _____ (watch) the tennis. It's very exciting.

5 Andy _____ (not play) very well at the moment.

6 I _____ (not know) where my phone is.

7 It's always hot in tropical countries, it _____ (not snow) there.

8 What _____ (you / study) this year?

5 Complete the article with the best answer, A, B, C or D, for each space.

Subject: **Antonio**

Antonio comes from Mexico, but at the moment he 1) _____ English in Brighton. He 2) _____ with an English family for three months. He 3) _____ the family very much, but he 4) _____ the weather in England.

Antonio says:

'When it's sunny, we 5) _____ to the beach and swim in the sea, but I 6) _____ today because it's too cold. It 7) _____ in England, so we 8) _____ a lot of time outdoors.

'Tonight, I 9) _____ dinner for my English family. I 10) _____ English food, because the family wants to try a traditional Mexican meal. I 11) _____ at home, so today I 12) _____ a recipe book.'

GOLD EXPERIENCE

1 **A** studies **(B)** is studying
   C doesn't study **D** isn't studying
2 **A** stays **B** is staying
   C doesn't stay **D** isn't staying
3 **A** likes **B** is liking
   C doesn't like **D** isn't liking
4 **A** likes **B** is liking
   C doesn't like **D** isn't liking
5 **A** go **B** are going
   C don't go **D** aren't going
6 **A** swim **B** am swimming
   C don't swim **D** 'm not swimming
7 **A** often rains **B** is often raining
   C doesn't often rain **D** isn't often raining
8 **A** spend **B** are spending
   C don't spend **D** aren't spending
9 **A** make **B** 'm making
   C don't make **D** 'm not making
10 **A** cook **B** 'm cooking
   C don't cook **D** 'm not cooking
11 **A** usually cook **B** 'm usually cooking
   C don't usually cook **D** 'm not usually cooking
12 **A** use **B** 'm using
   C don't use **D** 'm not using

Time expressions

6 **Rewrite the sentences with the word in brackets in the correct place.**

1 We play football in the park in the afternoon. (usually)
   We usually play football in the park in the afternoon.

2 It snows in the desert. (never)

3 They laugh all the time. They are serious. (never)

4 We meet our friends after school. (often)

5 I get up early. (most days)

6 Is she rude? (always)

7 **Complete the text with these time expressions.**

every weekend ~~most days~~
now and then once a week
twice a year usually

💬 View previous comments   Cancel Share Post

I'm fed up with homework! I spend two hours doing it 1) *most days* and I have to complete a project 2) _____ . I really hate working on Saturday and Sunday.
My favourite subject is drama. We have drama lessons 3) _____ , on Friday afternoon. The drama group puts on a play
4) _____ – in December and June. We
5) _____ perform a classical play, but
6) _____ we write our own play.

Write a comment   Support

8 **Write sentences and questions. Use the present simple or present continuous.**

1 What / you / usually / do / after school / ?
   What do you usually do after school?

2 They / often / speak / Spanish / at home

3 It / rain / here. What / be / the / weather / like / there / ?

4 It / not / often snow / in the winter here

5 We / wait / for / the bus / to go into town

6 I / not enjoy / the party, so / I / go / home

7 Please / not interrupt / me / when / I / listen / to a programme

8 I / not watch / TV / because / I / cook / dinner

VOCABULARY

1 Complete the sentences with the correct language and communication words. The first letter has been given.

1 Do you s _p e a k_ Arabic?
2 Listen and I'll tell you how to p.. this word.
3 Please can you e.. what to do?
4 It isn't easy to t.. poems from a different language.
5 Do you u.. the text?
6 I didn't hear you. Can you r.. that, please?

2 Choose the correct words.

1 _Listen_/Hear! This is important information.
2 What language do they _talk/speak_ in Egypt?
3 I _understand/translate_ Russian, but find it difficult to read.
4 Don't _say/tell_ me the answer. I want to work it out for myself.
5 What did you _pronounce/say_?
6 Can you _repeat/tell_ the words? I didn't hear the difference.
7 Let me _speak/explain_ how to send a text message.
8 Do you _mean/say_ you don't know or you won't tell me?

3 Complete the crossword.

(Crossword grid with answers: 3 Across PRONOUNCE, with numbered cells 1 T, 2 M, 3 P, 4 U, 5 S, 6 E, 7 L, 8 T, 9 S, 10 H, 11 T, 12 R)

Across

3 say a word with the correct sounds
4 know what something means
6 tell someone about something so they can understand it
8 to say things as part of a conversation
9 to speak words
10 to know that a sound is being made
12 to say or do something again

Down

1 change words from one language to another language
2 to have a meaning, definition or explanation
5 to talk to people; to say and understand words of a language
7 pay attention to what someone is saying or a sound
11 give information

4 Choose the correct answer, A, B, C or D.

1 Thank you for _____ me.
  A talking   (B) telling
  C speaking   D saying

2 Who were you _____ to on the phone?
  A hearing   B saying
  C telling   D talking

3 I'm sorry, I can't _____ you because it's too noisy here.
  A talk   B listen
  C hear   D tell

4 What did you _____?
  A say   B tell
  C talk   D listen

5 Do you want to _____ to music or watch a film?
  A speak   B listen
  C hear   D say

6 Do you _____ to your friends about your problems?
  A say   B hear
  C talk   D tell

5 Complete the sentences with *about* or *to*.

1 The teacher is speaking _____*to*_____ the class.
2 She's speaking _____ learning languages.
3 She's telling them _____ her experience of living in different countries.
4 She's trying to explain the situation _____ them.
5 Are they listening _____ her?
6 Look, Holly is talking _____ Aiden. I didn't know they were friends.
7 What are they talking _____?

6 Match the sentence beginnings (1–6) with the endings (A–F).

1 I can't read the article aloud _D_
2 They speak very quietly _____
3 It's difficult to translate poetry _____
4 I want to remember the words _____
5 They didn't understand the first time _____
6 It's difficult to explain on the phone _____

A so I'm explaining it again.
B because the sound is as important as the meaning.
C because you can't see the picture.
D because I don't know how to pronounce the words.
E so I'm repeating them many times.
F so it's hard to hear what they're saying.

7 Complete the text with these verbs.

> pronounce   repeat   say   ~~speak~~
> translate   understand

View previous comments   Cancel   Share   Post

Here I am in Beijing. I'm travelling in China for three months. I'm learning to
1) _____*speak*_____ Chinese, but people often don't
2) _____ what I 3) _____.
I use my hands a lot, I point at things and I 4) _____ everything several times. Finally, I ask my friend to
5) _____ for me. The problem is that I don't
6) _____ the words correctly. Chinese is a very difficult language!

8 Replace the underlined words in the review with these words.

> ~~delicious~~   disgusting   fantastic   furious
> hilarious   huge

Excelsior

Excelsior   **Overall rating: ***

The website described the food at the restaurant as
1) very nice _____*delicious*_____ , so we were expecting to have a 2) very good _____ evening there.
We arrived at eight o'clock. The restaurant was
3) very big _____ and there weren't many people there. We soon found out the reason. The waiters mixed up the orders and brought us the wrong things. At first, we thought it was 4) very funny _____ , but we stopped laughing when we got the food. It was
5) very bad _____ . Then we got the bill.
The meal was extremely expensive and we didn't think it was funny at all. In fact we were
6) very angry _____ .

GRAMMAR

Past simple

1 Rewrite the sentences in the past simple.

1 Entering the talent competition is a very good idea.

   Entering the talent competition was a very good idea.

2 I am not confident about winning.

3 The prizes aren't very interesting.

4 This competition is a chance to change my life.

5 The judges are the most important people.

6 Are you the winner?

2 Complete the table with the past simple form of the verbs.

carry	1)	*carried*
come	2)	
have	3)	
move	4)	
plan	5)	
remember	6)	
study	7)	
win	8)	

3 Complete the text with the past simple form of the verbs in brackets.

Christopher Columbus

Christopher Columbus 1) ___*travelled*___ (travel) from Europe across the Atlantic Ocean and
2) _____ (find) a new world. When he
3) _____ (leave) Spain in 1492, Europeans
4) _____ (not know) about America.
Columbus 5) _____ (want) to find a new way to India. It 6) _____ (take) him five weeks to cross the ocean. He 7) _____ (not expect) to discover America. After their long journey, he and his men 8) _____ (believe) they were in India.

4 Write questions.

1 Amelia told Stephen about the party.
   Did Amelia tell Stephen about the party?

2 You visited England last year.

3 James worked in a Turkish restaurant.

4 James studied languages at school.

5 You went to the cinema yesterday evening.

6 You explained how to play the game.

7 They were at home last night.

8 It was a good idea to tell them about the trip.

Past simple and past continuous

5 Complete the sentences with the past continuous form of the verbs in brackets.

1 I ___was studying___ (study) Turkish last year.
2 They _____ (tell) me about their home town.
3 He _____ (not speak) Spanish.
4 They _____ (not listen) to you.
5 Where _____ (Aiden / go)?
6 Who _____ (they / expect) to meet?
7 She _____ (watch) an interesting programme.
8 We _____ (not enjoy) the party.
9 Who _____ (you / talk) to?

6 Complete the sentences with the past continuous form of these verbs.

~~cook~~   listen   play   send   take   watch

At four o'clock on Saturday afternoon,
1 Daniel ___was cooking___ pasta.
2 Harry _____ photos.
3 Max and Isla _____ chess.
4 Holly and Ella _____ to music.
5 Lily and Emily _____ TV.
6 Jacob _____ a text message.

7 Choose the correct words.

1 Columbus *tried/was trying* to find a new way to India when he *discovered/was discovering* America.
2 What *were they talking/did they talk* about when I *came/was coming* into the room?
3 They *didn't speak/weren't speaking* to us in Spanish while we *stayed/were staying* with them.
4 When we *arrived/were arriving*, all the guests *danced/were dancing*.
5 I *waited/was waiting* at the bus stop when I *saw/was seeing* the accident.
6 I *didn't use/wasn't using* my phone while I *travelled/was travelling*.

8 Complete the conversation with the correct past form of the verbs in brackets.

Granddad

Why 1) ___didn't you take___ (you / not take) a camera, a map or a guidebook on your holiday?

Ella

I didn't need them. I just 2) _____ (put) my smart phone in my pocket. When I 3) _____ (sightsee), I 4) _____ (use) my phone as a camera. When I 5) _____ (look) for somewhere to eat, my phone 6) _____ (become) a guidebook.

Granddad

I see! So you 7) _____ (not carry) a heavy bag.

Ella

Right! That's why I 8) _____ (not get) tired while I 9) _____ (visit) different places.

Revision Units 1 – 2

VOCABULARY

1 Complete the descriptions with these words.

about   at (x4)   in   ~~of~~   with

I'm frightened 1) ___of___ speaking in public and I don't like parties because I'm not good 2) _____ talking to people I don't know. I prefer to listen to other people. I don't like to say what I think, in case people disagree with me.

Ava

I love playing tennis and football. I get excited 3) _____ competitions. I don't understand how people can sit still. I always want to run and dance. I love parties, I play the saxophone and I get fed up 4) _____ people telling me to be quiet!

Evie

He works hard and gets good grades. He's interested 5) _____ learning new things and quick to understand new information. He is brilliant 6) _____ explaining things to his classmates, too. He likes organising people and telling them what to do.

Charlie

Daniel

He enjoys making people laugh and is good 7) _____ telling jokes. He is bad 8) _____ listening in class, so he doesn't hear the teacher's questions. He doesn't apologise. He is often late for school and doesn't always do his homework.

2 Read the descriptions in Exercise 1 again and complete the sentences. The first letter has been given.

Ava is 1) s _h_ _y_ . She isn't
2) c_____ .
Evie is 3) s_____ and
4) n_____ .
Charlie is 5) b_____ .
He's 6) c_____ .
Daniel is 7) f_____ , but he's 8) l_____ .

3 Choose the correct words.

1 Please *hear*/*listen to* what I'm *saying*/*talking*.
2 Can you *explain*/*translate* what you *understand*/*mean*?
3 What did they *tell*/*speak* you?
4 How do you *pronounce*/*repeat* this word? I don't know how to *speak*/*say* it.
5 I don't *explain*/*understand* what you're *talking*/*telling* about.
6 Can you *speak*/*translate* this word? I don't know what it *means*/*pronounces*.
7 Can you *repeat*/*talk* that, please, I didn't *listen to*/*hear* you?
8 I enjoy *listening to*/*hearing* my grandfather *talking*/*telling* stories.

GOLD EXPERIENCE

GRAMMAR

1 Complete the text with the correct form of the verbs in brackets.

💬 View previous comments   Cancel   Share   Post

I usually 1) _speak_ (speak) Spanish at home, but today I 2) _____ (speak) English, because my friend from England
3) _____ (stay) with me.
He 4) _____ (come) to school with me every day, because he 5) _____ (learn) Spanish. There are a lot of words he
6) _____ (not know), so I
7) _____ (translate) the words and
8) _____ (explain) the grammar.
My English 9) _____ (improve), but his Spanish 10) _____ (not get) better!

2 Write questions.

1 What language / Felipe / usually / speak / ?
   What language does Felipe usually speak?

2 Why / he / not speak / Spanish today / ?

3 Why / Felipe's friend / stay / with him / ?

4 Where / Felipe and William / go every day / ?

5 Why / Felipe / translate / a lot of words / ?

6 Why / William's Spanish / not get / better / ?

3 Rewrite the sentences in the past simple.

1 Felipe and William are good friends.
   Felipe and William were good friends.

2 Felipe takes William to visit his friends.

3 Does William go to school with Felipe?

4 Felipe and William speak English all the time.

5 Why don't Felipe and William speak Spanish?

6 William doesn't speak Spanish very well.

7 Felipe translates the words William doesn't know.

8 William stops trying to speak Spanish.

4 Complete the sentences with the past simple form of the verbs in brackets. Put the time expressions in the correct place in the sentences.

1 We _____ (have) a holiday when I _____ (be) a child. (every year)
   We had a holiday every year when I was a child.

2 We _____ (spend) holidays at the beach. (often)

3 I _____ (go) swimming. (most days)

4 My parents _____ (buy) me an ice cream. (usually)

5 My sister and I _____ (find) interesting animals on the beach. (now and then)

6 We _____ (take) them home. (never)

7 We _____ (be) happy to go to the beach. (always)

8 We _____ (play) beach games. (sometimes)

5 Choose the correct words.

Mountain Adventure
One day last summer my brother and I were walking in the mountains when the weather suddenly
1) **changed**/was changing. One minute it was hot and sunny, the next it 2) **rained/was raining** very hard. We were wearing T-shirts and shorts. We
3) **didn't have/weren't having** any warm clothes with us. We 4) **ran/were running** down the mountain to find shelter when my brother
5) **fell/was falling** over and hurt his leg.
While we 6) **tried/were trying** to call for help, we
7) **dropped/were dropping** our mobile phone and the screen broke. Luckily, our parents 8) **already came/were already coming** to find us. We were very happy to see them!

03 Sounds of the future

VOCABULARY

1 Match 1–6 with a–f to make compound nouns.

1	air	a	dryer
2	dish	b	conditioning
3	electricity	c	machine
4	hair	d	phones
5	head	e	supply
6	washing	f	washer

2 Complete the sentences with these words.

> dishwasher   fridge   hair straighteners
> ~~iron~~   microwave   plug   speakers
> washing machine

1 My shirt is clean and dry and now I need to use the _____iron_____.
2 Let's use the _____ so we can all hear the music.
3 Put the butter in the _____ to keep it cool.
4 You can heat food quickly in the _____.
5 Which _____ is for the computer?
6 I use _____ because I don't like my curly hair.
7 Dirty clothes go in the _____.
8 All the plates and cups in the _____ are clean. Please put them away.

3 Answer the questions.

1 Where do you put dirty cups and plates?
   _____In the dishwasher_____
2 Where do you put food to keep it fresh?
   _____
3 What do you use to dry your hair?
   _____
4 What do you use to connect a machine to the electricity supply?
   _____
5 What do you use to keep a room cool?
   _____
6 Where do you put dirty clothes?
   _____

4 Complete the email. The first letter of each word has been given.

Subject: **My holiday!**

Hi Grace
I'm on holiday in Spain. We're staying at a lovely house, but yesterday the 1) e*lectricity* s*upply* failed and all the machines in the house stopped working! I washed my hair, but I couldn't use the 2) h_____ to dry it. We couldn't heat any food because the 3) m_____ wasn't working and the food in the 4) f_____ went bad. We had to wash the plates by hand because we couldn't use the 5) d_____. We haven't got anything to wear because our clothes are in the 6) w_____ m_____ and they're still dirty. I didn't know how much we needed electricity!
Hope you get this message!
Charlotte

5 **Match the sentence beginnings (1–6) with the endings (A–F).**

1 The pictures on ___C___
2 I put my food _____
3 I use hair straighteners _____
4 I switched on the air conditioning _____
5 We used the microwave _____
6 Put your dirty plate _____

A because the room was very hot.
B in the dishwasher, please.
C our new 3D TV are great.
D because I don't like curly hair.
E in the fridge to keep it fresh.
F to heat our pizzas.

6 **Choose the correct phrasal verbs.**

1 Remember to *switch off*/turn down/plug in the lights when you go out.
2 Can you *turn up/turn down/switch on* the TV, it's too loud.
3 We can't get any more plates in, so please *switch on/turn up/plug in* the dishwasher.
4 Please *plug in/turn up/pick up* your dirty clothes and put them in the washing machine.
5 I need to *switch off/plug in/turn down* my hairdryer to dry my hair.
6 Please *pick up/switch on/turn up* the oven, it isn't hot enough.
7 *Switch on/Plug in/Switch off* the computer, we aren't using it now.
8 Don't *plug in/switch on/turn down* the washing machine, I want to put some more clothes in it.

7 **Complete the crossword.**

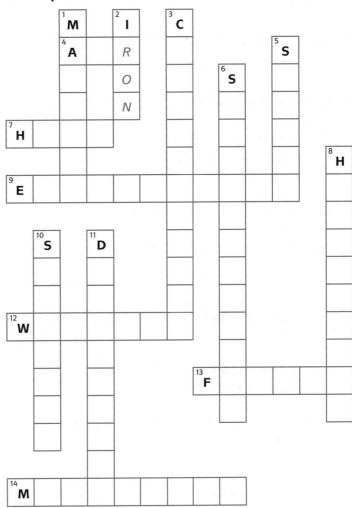

Across

4, 3 down If a room is very hot, you need _____.
7, 6 down Use these if you don't want curly hair.
9, 5 down Plug in the computer to connect it to the _____.
12, 1 down Switch on the _____ to wash your clothes.
13 Keep food in the _____.
14 Heat food in the _____.

Down

1 See 12 across.
2 Wash and dry your clothes and then use the _____.
3 See 4 across.
5 See 9 across.
6 See 7 across.
8 Use your _____ to listen to your MP3 player.
10 Turn up the _____ so we can hear the music.
11 Clear the table and put the plates in the _____.

GRAMMAR

Talking about the future: *will, going to*

1 Put the words in the correct order to make sentences.

1 Technology / going / to / is / change / lives / our / .
Technology is going to change our lives.

2 your / birthday / I'll / a cake / for / make / .

3 washing machine / Will / switch on / you / the / ?

4 to write / We / a shopping list / won't / need / .

5 will / The / fridge / text message / us / send / a / .

6 I'm / air conditioning / going / to / turn on / not / the / .

7 They / tomorrow / are / to / buy / new / a computer game / going / .

8 headphones / you / Are / to / buy / some / new / going / ?

2 Choose the correct words.

Lucy: What 1) *are you going to/will you* do at the weekend?

Mia: 2) *I'm going to/I'll* meet my friend Ella in town on Saturday. We plan to look round the shops.

Lucy: 3) *Are you going to/Will you* buy some new clothes?

Mia: Yes, I expect 4) *we're going to/we will*.

Lucy: Sounds great! 5) *I'm going to/I'll* come with you!

Mia: 6) *I'm not going to/I won't* take a lot of money, because I don't want to spend too much.

Lucy: I agree, 7) *I'm not going to/I won't* spend a lot of money, either.

Mia: OK, let's go together. 8) *Are you going to/Will you* call me when you're ready to leave?

Lucy: Yes, and 9) *I'm going to/I'll* meet you at the station.

Mia: OK, 10) *I'm going to/I'll* buy the tickets.

3 Complete the sentences with the correct form of *will* or *going to*.

1 It's really hot in here. OK, I _____'ll_____ turn up the air conditioning.

2 We can help you tidy up. We _____ put the dirty plates in the dishwasher.

3 Harry's hungry, so he _____ heat up a pizza.

4 When we get a smart fridge, we _____ run out of food.

5 What _____ (you) see at the cinema?

6 I _____ buy a new computer game tomorrow.

7 _____ (you) help me with my homework?

8 _____ (Oscar) show us his photos tonight?

4 Complete the conversation with the correct forms of *will* or *going to* and the verbs in brackets.

Jake: Hi, Harry, where are you going?

Harry: To the computer shop. I 1) *'m going to buy* (buy) a new game.

Jake: OK, I 2) _____ (come) with you.

Harry: The games are in order, so it 3) _____ (not take) long to find the one I want.

Jake: There are no prices on these games. I 4) _____ (ask) how much they cost.

Shop assistant: They're 10 euros today, but we 5) _____ (have) a sale next week, so these games 6) _____ (cost) 8 euros.

Harry: Thanks! I 7) _____ (not buy) the game today. I 8) _____ (wait) until next week.

someone, anyone, everyone, no one, something, anything, everything, nothing

5 **Rewrite the sentences. Replace the underlined words with a single word.**

1 They didn't put <u>any of the things</u> in the drawer.
  They didn't put anything in the drawer.

2 We told <u>all the people</u> what to do.

3 I saw <u>a person</u> take your phone.

4 <u>None of the people</u> offered to help.

5 The cat pushed <u>a thing</u> off the shelf.

6 They used a lot of plates and cups and they left <u>all of the things</u> dirty.

6 **Choose the correct words.**

Subject: **Yesterday**

Hey Ava
You missed a fun event yesterday! I was at the shopping mall when I noticed that 1) *everyone/ someone/everything* was waiting for 2) *anything/ nothing/something* to happen. At first, 3) *anyone/ no one/nothing* moved, then 4) *someone/anyone/ everyone* began to dance and, one by one, we all joined in until 5) *anyone/everyone/someone* was dancing. Then, suddenly the music stopped, and 6) *anything/something/everything* was quiet again. Why don't you come to the mall next Saturday? Maybe there'll be another surprise event!
See you
Jake

7 **Complete the sentences with these words.**

> anyone   anything   everyone   ~~everything~~
> no one   nothing   someone   something

1 Are you ready to start? Have you got __*everything*__ you need?

2 There were a lot of people there, but _____ spoke to me.

3 We won't start until _____ is sitting down.

4 There's _____ missing, but I'm not sure what it is.

5 The room is locked. Does _____ have the key?

6 The box is empty, there's _____ in it.

7 I can't manage on my own. I need _____ to help me carry this heavy bag.

8 Are you hungry? Can I get you _____ to eat?

8 **Complete the conversation. Use one word in each space.**

Lily: We're going to have a party at the end of term.

Jessica: 1) __*Everyone*__ in our class will be invited and we'll do 2) _____ ourselves.

Max: OK, I'll write the invitations.

Lily: Great! Make sure 3) _____ is left out.

Max: Has 4) _____ got a pen?

Lily: Next, 5) _____ needs to buy the food and drink.

Alfie: OK, I'll do that.

Lily: Thanks, Alfie. So, I think 6) _____ has got 7) _____ to do.

Alfie: Yes, that's right. Max is going to write the invitations. I'm going to buy the food and drink.

Max: Is there 8) _____ else to do?

Jessica: Yes, the music! I'll look after the music.

Lily: Great, now there's 9) _____ left to organise.

All: We're going to have a great time!

VOCABULARY

1 Find the odd word out in each group.

1 fail	pass	take	teach
2 examiner	learner	lesson	teacher
3 classroom	timetable	library	corridor
4 test	exam	lesson	grade
5 exam	learn	revise	teach
6 practise	teacher	revise	study
7 skill	miss	fail	pass
8 practise	revise	curriculum	study

2 Choose the correct words.

1 Check your *curriculum/timetable* to see what lessons you have each week and what time your lessons are each day.

2 We have *a break/an exam* between lessons in the morning.

3 One important *grade/rule* in our school is that you mustn't run in the *corridor/exam*.

4 In an oral test, the *examiner/learner* asks you questions and gives you a grade.

5 I'll get my exam results next week. I hope I *pass/take* them.

6 Did you *fail/revise* for the test today?

3 Complete the text with these words.

> ~~curriculum~~ fail grades learn pass
> practise revise teach tests timetable

The 1) *curriculum* sets out all the subjects you have to 2) .... at school. You take exams at the end of the year. It's important to 3) .... the exams. For the last few weeks before the exams, the 4) .... changes. The teachers don't 5) .... any new material, you just 6) .... everything you learnt in the year. You do 7) .... in school to prepare for the exams and to see whether you are likely to get good 8) .... It's important to 9) .... for the exams, because you don't want to 10) .... them.

4 Complete the notice. Use one word in each space.

Plan for success

Do you want to 1) _____pass_____ your exams?
Follow these 2) .... and you will get good 3) ....
It's important to 4) ...., so make time to study every day.
Make a 5) .... for your revision, with time for each subject.
Don't work for a long time without taking a 6) .... Little and often is the best way to learn.

5 Find and write ten adverbs.

c	l	e	a	r	l	y	r	e
h	a	s	l	o	x	r	e	a
h	a	r	d	i	s	y	g	s
a	q	u	e	l	o	y	u	i
p	f	t	o	f	w	e	l	l
p	f	a	s	t	u	k	a	y
i	c	m	n	o	p	l	r	p
l	s	l	o	w	l	y	l	y
y	q	u	i	c	k	l	y	y

1 ....*clearly*....   2 ....
3 ....   4 ....
5 ....   6 ....
7 ....   8 ....
9 ....   10 ....

6 Choose the correct words.

1 Read the instructions *careful*/*carefully* because it's *easy*/*easily* to make a mistake.

2 It's a *good*/*well* idea to practise *regular*/*regularly*.

3 Harry is able to learn lessons *quick*/*quickly* and explain them *clear*/*clearly*.

4 Holly will be *happy*/*happily* to help you, if you ask her *nice*/*nicely*.

5 Aiden left early, but he walks very *slow*/*slowly*, so I'll *easy*/*easily* catch up with him.

6 The key to doing *good*/*well* in your exam is *careful*/*carefully* planning.

7 Jack's writing is *clear*/*clearly* and *easy*/*easily* to read.

8 Jessica smiled *happy*/*happily* when she heard that her grades were *good*/*well*.

7 Complete the text with the correct form of these adjectives.

~~clear~~   easy   fast   good (x2)   hard (x2)
quick   regular (x2)

> 💬 View previous comments   Cancel   Share   Post
>
> I'm learning to play the guitar. Three months ago, I bought a book called *How to play the guitar*. The pages are set out very 1) *clearly* and the instructions are 2) _____ to follow. At first I made 3) _____ progress. The book says 4) _____ practice is important and I played every day. So, in the beginning, I was working 5) _____ and I was learning 6) _____. However, I 7) _____ got bored with the songs in the book. It's 8) _____ to play songs you don't really like, so I stopped practising 9) _____. Then I joined a band. I wanted to play 10) _____ because the other musicians were brilliant.
>
> Write a comment   Support

8 Read Suzy's advice and choose the best answer, A, B or C, for each space.

Dear Suzy

> Dear Suzy,
>
> Can you help me?
>
> I'm trying to train my dog, but it isn't 1) _____ to explain things to a dog. The problem is, I don't think my dog is very 2) _____. It doesn't learn 3) _____!
>
> Holly

Suzy Says

Hi Holly,
You have to practise 4) _____.
Be 5) _____ to plan a training lesson every day. It's a 6) _____ idea to keep the lessons short, so the dog doesn't get bored. Try to be 7) _____ and remember to speak 8) _____ to the dog.

	A	B	C
1	easily	(B) easy	hard
2	clever	cleverly	fast
3	quick	quickly	hard
4	regular	well	regularly
5	careful	carefully	clear
6	well	hard	good
7	quick	quickly	hard
8	soft	quiet	quietly

GRAMMAR

Making comparisons

1 Complete the table with the comparatives of these adjectives.

bad	1)	*worse*
big	2)	
clever	3)	
difficult	4)	
easy	5)	
fast	6)	
fit	7)	
good	8)	
nervous	9)	
nice	10)	

2 Complete the questions with the correct form of these adjectives.

> clear   easy   far   ~~fast~~   good   hard
> high   loud

Can you

1 … write as ___*fast*___ as you can speak?
2 … play the piano as _____ as you can sing?
3 … hit the ball as _____ as you can kick it?
4 … remember numbers as _____ as you can remember words?
5 … shout as _____ as you can whistle?
6 … swim as _____ as you can walk?
7 … jump as _____ as you can climb?
8 … see as _____ at night as you can see in the daytime?

3 Write comparative sentences.

1 library / gym (quiet)
> *The library is quieter than the gym.*
> *The gym isn't as quiet as the library.*

2 riding a bike / running (fast)

3 calling on the phone / texting (expensive)

4 reading / writing (easy)

5 school hall / classroom (big)

6 playing the game / winning (important)

7 rock climbing / ice skating (dangerous)

8 dancing / scuba diving (safe)

9 revising regularly / revising for a long time (good)

4 Write sentences. Use *too* or *not enough*.

1 We're going to be late. You / walk / quick
> *You aren't walking quickly enough.*

2 Your work is very bad. You / try / hard

3 I can't reach the top shelf. I / be tall

4 I can't carry this bag. It / be heavy

5 She won't help at all. She / be lazy

6 Your playing won't improve because you / practise

7 I can't reach the top shelf. It / be high

8 I can't carry this bag. I / be strong

9 Be quiet. You / speak / loud

10 Hurry up. You / walk / slow

5 Complete the sentences with a comparative form of these words.

> big   dangerous   ~~noisy~~   quiet
> safe   small

1 We can't revise at home, because it's *too noisy*.

2 It's not ___ to revise at home.

3 We can't cycle to school because the road is ___.

4 It's not ___ to cycle to school.

5 The TV won't fit in here. The cupboard is ___.

6 It's not ___.

Present continuous and present simple for future use and *shall*

6 Write sentences. Use the present continuous.

1 I / come / to see you tomorrow
   I'm coming to see you tomorrow.

2 We / take / our maths exam next week

3 We / have / pizza for lunch on Saturday

4 Isla and Max / watch / the film with us tonight / ?

5 You / not learn / to swim next term

6 Jacob / play / chess tomorrow

7 Choose the correct words.

1 My Dad *drives/is driving* me to school tomorrow.
2 The bus to town *leaves/is leaving* at 4.30.
3 *I don't take/I'm not taking* the bus into town this afternoon.
4 *Shall we/Do we* watch a DVD tonight?
5 *They show/They're showing* a new film at the cinema next Saturday.
6 School *starts/is starting* at 8.30 every day next year.
7 *Do I/Shall I* help you with your homework?
8 *We have/We're having* a party tonight.

8 Complete the conversation with the correct form of the verbs in brackets.

Amy: Hi, Holly, I checked the timetable. The train 1) ___*leaves*___ (leave) at half past three tomorrow.

Holly: Hi, Amy. OK, 2) ___ (I / buy) the tickets online?

Amy: Yes, that's a good idea. I'll tell Jon we 3) ___ (meet) at the station at three o'clock because he's always late.

Amy: My dad 4) ___ (drive) me to the station. 5) ___ (we / pick) you up?

Holly: Great! Thank you! What time 6) ___ (you / come) to my house?

Amy: At quarter to three. The train takes half an hour, so we 7) ___ (get) to town around four o'clock.

Holly: And the film 8) ___ (start) at four thirty. Perfect!

Revision Units 3 – 4

VOCABULARY

1 Complete the sentences with one or two words in each space. The first letter has been given.

1 It's very hot here, so we need a _ir conditioning_ .

2 My hair's wet. Can I borrow your h_____?

3 This is a silk shirt, so make sure the i_____ isn't too hot.

4 Please put the dirty plates in the d_____.

5 I need to connect the speakers to the electricity supply, but there isn't a p_____.

6 All your dirty clothes are in the w_____.

7 You won't hear the music if I use my h_____.

8 I use h_____ because I don't want my hair to be curly.

9 I'll heat your dinner in the m_____.

10 The butter is in the f_____.

2 Complete the sentences with a suitable phrasal verb.

1 You left your bedroom light on.
You forgot to _switch off_ your bedroom light.

2 Your dirty clothes are on the floor.
I want you to _____ your dirty clothes.

3 I need to connect the iron to the electricity supply.
I need to _____ the iron.

4 I want to watch a TV programme.
Please _____ the TV.

5 I can't hear the radio.
Please _____ the radio.

6 The music is too loud.
Please _____ the music.

3 Complete the crossword.

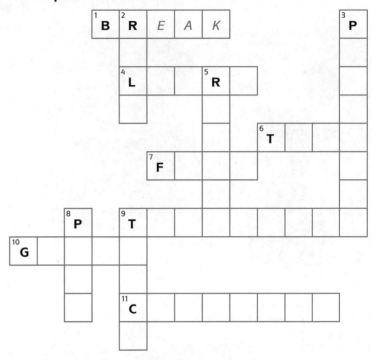

Across
1 A time between lessons
4 To have lessons
6 A list of questions that checks how much students know
7 To be unsuccessful in an exam
9 A list of lessons and times for each day of the week
10 The mark that a teacher gives for school work
11 A long narrow area in a building, with rooms on each side

Down
2 Something you must or mustn't do
3 To do exercises
5 To study for a test or an exam
8 To be successful in an exam
9 To give lessons to

GRAMMAR

1 Complete the text with the correct forms of *going to* or *will* and the verbs in brackets.

💬 View previous comments   Cancel   Share   Post

My brother, my sister and I are all 1) *going to learn* (learn) some new skills this year.
Oliver 2) _____ (learn) to play the drums.
He says he 3) _____ (work) very hard.
He's made a timetable and he 4) _____ (practise) regularly.
Sophie wants to learn to dance. Her friend from Hawaii says she 5) _____ (teach) her hula dancing. They 6) _____ (not do) anything else, they 7) _____ (spend) all their time dancing!
I 8) _____ (study) Japanese. I know I 9) _____ (find) it hard to learn because I'm not good at languages. I know learning Japanese 10) _____ (not be) easy because the alphabet is so different. It will take a long time, but I 11) _____ (not give up).

Write a comment   Support

2 Complete the sentences with these words.

> anyone   ~~anything~~   everyone   everything
> no one   nothing   someone   something

1 You aren't allowed to take ___*anything*___ into the exam room to help you, no dictionaries, calculators or mobile phones.
2 You must leave _____ on the table outside the exam room – all your bags, phones and dictionaries.
3 Is there _____ in the office?
4 I hope that _____ will answer the phone.
5 Make sure that there's _____ in your bag or your pockets.
6 There's _____ here. The room is empty.
7 You'll have to wait a long time, so take _____ to read.
8 Is _____ here now or are we still waiting for some more people?

3 Write comparative sentences.

1 Heating food in an oven / not / fast / heating food in a microwave
   Heating food in an oven isn't as fast as heating food in a microwave.
2 Checking words in a printed dictionary / not / quick / checking words online
3 Is watching films on 3D TV / good / watching films on ordinary TV / ?
4 My new headphones / not / comfortable / my old ones
5 The robot vacuum cleaner / quiet / the old vacuum cleaner
6 A mobile phone / not / expensive / a computer

4 Write sentences with *too* or *enough*.

1 The iron / be hot. It burned my shirt.
   The iron was too hot. It burned my shirt.
2 Put the pizza in the microwave. It / not be warm
3 Turn the music down. It / be loud
4 The food isn't fresh. The fridge / not be cold
5 I don't want to watch the film. It / not be interesting
6 We can't buy a 3D TV because it / be expensive

5 Choose the correct verbs.

Max: 1) *I visit/I'm visiting* the technology fair at the weekend. What 2) *do you do/are you doing*?

Lucy: 3) *I don't do/I'm not doing* anything special.

Max: Do you want to come with me? 4) *Shall/Will* I get another ticket?

Lucy: OK, yes, I'd like to come. What time?

Max: The exhibition 5) *opens/is opening* at nine o'clock, but 6) *I don't plan/I'm not planning* to get there early. 7) *I leave/I'm leaving* home at 9.30. 8) *I cycle/I'm cycling*, so it will take me about half an hour.

Lucy: OK, let's meet there, around ten o'clock.

Max: I want to see the food technology show. 9) *They explain/They're explaining* how listening to different sounds changes the way food tastes. 10) *It starts/It's starting* at eleven o'clock.

Lucy: OK, see you on Saturday.

23

Go for it!

VOCABULARY

1 Complete the crossword.

Across
1 Try to win against
4 Person who trains the team
7 Competition where you try to go faster than others
8 What the winner gets
9 Move the racket against

Down
1 Place to play tennis
2 Sports event between two people or teams
3 _____ a goal
5 Get more points than your opponent
6 Be the best in the game

Crossword grid:
1 ACROSS: C O M P E T E
2 Down: M
3 Down: S
4 Across: C
5 Down: B
6 Across/Down: W
7 Across: R
8 Across: P
9 Across: H

2 Match the verbs (1–6) with the nouns (a–f).

1 beat   a a match
2 hit   b a goal
3 play   c an opponent
4 run   d a prize
5 score   e a ball
6 win   f a race

3 Complete the sentences with these words.

> changing rooms   kick   ~~locker~~   prize
> race   track   train

1 Everyone has a _____locker_____ in the _____ where they keep their sports clothes and equipment.
2 The running club meets at the _____ on Wednesday afternoon.
3 Did Evie run in the 400 metre _____ today?
4 To score a goal in football, you _____ the ball into the net.
5 Jacob won the running competition, so he got the _____ .
6 The new coach is helping us _____ for the competition.

4 Choose the correct words.

Max: What sports do you do at school, Isla?
Isla: I play tennis in the summer. I'm getting better, especially now that I've got a new 1) *board/racket*. We play on the 2) *court/track* at the sports centre and the coach is helping us to 3) *score/train*.
Max: How often do you play?
Isla: Every Friday. And next week I'm playing a 4) *match/race* against Holly. She 5) *beat/won* me last time we played because she 6) *hits/kicks* the ball really hard. I don't think I'll win a 7) *locker/prize*, but I'll enjoy playing. What about you?
Max: I'm doing sprint cycling. I've just got a new bike and a 8) *helmet/wetsuit*.

5 Complete the sentences with the correct sport words. The first letter has been given.

1 You need a h _e l m e t_ for sprint cycling.
2 The kiteboarding club will lend you a w_____ .
3 Evie bought a new r_____ to play tennis.
4 Boxers wear special g_____ .
5 You can hire a b_____ to go surfing.
6 Don't forget your g_____ for swimming.

6 Choose the correct answer, A, B, C or D.

1 Every year, schools in our town _____ against each other in sports events.
   A race   B score
   C compete   D beat

2 Let's play tennis this afternoon. I'll meet you at the tennis _____ .
   A match   B court
   C race   D prize

3 Did you watch the football _____ on Saturday?
   A score   B goal
   C competition   D match

4 Our new _____ has encouraged the team to train harder this year.
   A coach   B player
   C train   D winner

5 Ethan didn't _____ any goals today.
   A win   B hit
   C score   D kick

6 We have to _____ this match to stay in the competition.
   A beat   B compete
   C win   D lose

7 Harry ran the 10 km _____ in 45 minutes.
   A court   B match
   C track   D race

8 Do you think Isla will _____ Sophie?
   A win   B beat
   C compete   D match

7 Find the odd one out in each group.

1 helmet   race   racket   wetsuit
2 coach   court   locker   track
3 goggles   racket   surfboard   wetsuit
4 changing room   compete   kick   win
5 beat   hit   lose   prize
6 gloves   practise   score   train

8 Complete the email with these words.

> beat   coach   compete   court   ~~matches~~
>   practise   prizes   score

mailbox   Today | Mail | Calendar | Contacts

Reply | Reply All | Forward | Delete

From: Jake   Subject: Hi

Hi Mum
I'm really enjoying summer camp. You won't believe it, but I'm in the top tennis group! We play 1) _matches_ on the tennis 2) _____, but we 3) _____ by hitting the ball against the wall. Our 4) _____ says it's a good way to train. It's true that our group is the best. We 5) _____ the other groups and we win a lot of the 6) _____. But I think it's more fun to 7) _____ against my friends and to see who can 8) _____ more points.
Two more weeks to enjoy and then back to school!
Love
Jake

GRAMMAR

Present perfect simple

1 **Write sentences. Use the present perfect form of the verbs.**

1 I / play / in a lot of football matches this term
   I've played in a lot of football matches this term.

2 Our team / not win / any matches this year

3 I not / try / mud running, but I'd like to

4 You look hot. You / go / running / ?

5 You / put / your clothes in your locker / ?

6 Jacob / start / learning kickboxing with the new coach

7 The school / buy / some new footballs

8 They / stop / climbing because the wall isn't safe

2 **Rewrite the sentences with the adverbs in brackets in the correct place.**

1 The match has started. (just)
   The match has just started.

2 Sam has swum six lengths. (already)

3 Grace hasn't changed into her sports clothes. (yet)

4 Has the match started? (already)

5 Alfie has won the prize! (just)

6 The match hasn't finished. (yet).

7 We've joined the water polo team. (already)

8 They have found the key to the changing room. (just)

9 We haven't seen the new swimming pool. (yet)

3 **Look at the chart and write sentences. Use the present perfect form and *already/yet* where appropriate.**

	Jack	Amelia
decide to get fit	✓	✓
buy tennis rackets	✓	✓
join a club	✗	✗
have a tennis lesson	✗	✓
win a match	✓	✗

1 Jack and Amelia ___*have decided to get fit*___ .
2 They _____ .
3 They _____ .
4 Jack _____ .
5 Amelia _____ .
6 Jack _____ ,
   but Amelia _____ .

4 **Complete the blog with the present perfect form of the verbs in brackets.**

💬 View previous comments   Cancel   Share   Post

There are lots of new sports to try at the sports centre. They 1) *have just employed* (just / employ) some new coaches for kickboxing, tennis, water polo and sprint cycling. I'm good at swimming, so I 2) _____ (already / join) the water polo team, but we 3) _____ (not have / our first training session / yet). I'm interested in the sprint cycling, but I 4) _____ (not get / a bike / yet). The kickboxing coach 5) _____ (just / put up) the timetable and I 6) _____ (already / pay) for the first lesson.

Write a comment   Support

Past simple and present perfect simple

5 **Choose the correct form of the verbs.**

1 Yesterday's match _was_/_has been_ very exciting.

2 I _didn't run_/_hadn't run_ a race this afternoon.

3 I _cycled_/_have cycled_ to school today.

4 _Did the race finish_?/_Has the race finished_?

5 How many people _took_/_have taken_ part in the New York Marathon this year?

6 Our football team _trained_/_has trained_ really hard this year, so I hope they win.

7 We _didn't play_/_haven't played_ tennis for weeks!

8 _We just won_/_We've just won_ the competition!

6 **Write the responses in the conversation.**

Olivia: Hey, you two. Look at all the new sports we can do at the sports centre now.

Lucy: 1) You / try sprint cycling / ?
Have you tried sprint cycling?

Olivia: No, I haven't. I haven't got a bike. What about you?

Lucy: 2) I / try / sprint cycling / last week, but I / not like / it

Olivia: What about you, Dan?

Dan: 3) I / join / the water polo team

Olivia: Is it fun?

Dan: 4) We / have / a training session yesterday, but we / not play / a match yet

Lucy: Sounds great. Maybe we should join, too.

Olivia: 5) I never / play / water polo

Dan: Well, why don't you both come? We've got another training session this afternoon.

Lucy: 6) I not / finish / last week's homework yet

Olivia: I haven't got any homework. I'll come!

7 **Complete the sentences with the correct form of these verbs and the words in brackets.**

> buy   find   have   run   see   start
> ~~swim~~   try   win

1 We often swim in the pool, but we
've never swum (never) in the river before.

2 I don't think Thomas will complete the course, he _____ (never) a marathon before.

3 Our school _____ two prizes in the sports competition last week.

4 I _____ (just) some goggles, because I'm taking up synchronised swimming.

5 William lost his racket yesterday. _____ (he) it yet?

6 The match _____ at three o'clock.

7 Congratulations! This is the first time I _____ (ever) you win a race!

8 _____ (you ever) kickboxing?

9 I _____ my first swimming lesson yesterday.

8 **Complete the email with the correct form of the verbs in brackets.**

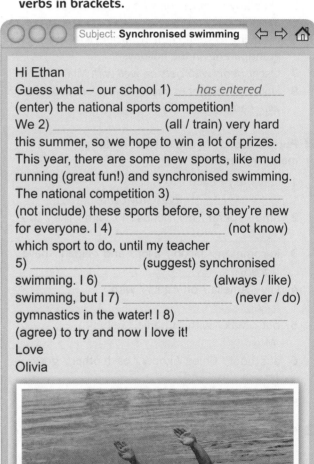

Subject: **Synchronised swimming**

Hi Ethan
Guess what – our school 1) _has entered_ (enter) the national sports competition!
We 2) _____ (all / train) very hard this summer, so we hope to win a lot of prizes. This year, there are some new sports, like mud running (great fun!) and synchronised swimming. The national competition 3) _____ (not include) these sports before, so they're new for everyone. I 4) _____ (not know) which sport to do, until my teacher 5) _____ (suggest) synchronised swimming. I 6) _____ (always / like) swimming, but I 7) _____ (never / do) gymnastics in the water! I 8) _____ (agree) to try and now I love it!
Love
Olivia

Getting on

VOCABULARY

1 **Choose the correct phrases and phrasal verbs.**

1 I'd like to be friends, I don't want to *get to know/fall out with* you.
2 It's better to *deal with/spend time with* the problem.
3 I'm sorry you've had *a lot in common/a hard time* recently.
4 Do you *get to know/have a lot in common* with your brothers and sisters?
5 Let's *stay calm/get on with each other* and talk about it.
6 I'm going to *spend time with/deal with* my grandparents in the holidays.
7 Oscar *deals with/gets on well with* Mia.
8 How did you *get to know/have a lot in common with* each other?

2 **Put the words in the correct order to make sentences.**

1 stay / Try / calm / to / .
Try to stay calm.
2 time / spend / my friends / I / with / like / to / .
3 in common / Jacob / a lot / and / Noah / have / .
Jacob
4 Lily / Amelia / on / gets / with / .
Lily
5 out / Max / with / Charlie / fell / .
Max
6 at school / Chloe / know / each other / got / Jessica / to / and / .
Chloe

3 **Replace the underlined phrases.**

> deal with   fall out with   get on with
> ~~get to know~~   a hard time
> have a lot in common
> spend time with   stay calm

1 I'd like to <u>become friends with</u> William, he seems interesting.
I'd like to get to know William, he seems interesting.

2 Holly is having <u>some difficult problems</u> at the moment.

3 I've got a problem at school and I don't know how to <u>find a way to stop</u> it.

4 You should <u>stop yourself getting upset or angry</u> and not shout at your brother.

5 I'd like to <u>be together with</u> you during the holidays.

6 My sister is older than me and we don't <u>share the same ideas or interests</u>.

7 I didn't want to <u>argue with</u> Ethan, but he was very rude to me.

8 Do you <u>have a good relationship with</u> your classmates?

4 **Complete the text with the best answer, A, B, C or D, for each space.**

My cousins, Sam and Eliza, live on the other side of the country, so I hardly ever see them and I didn't know them well. But during the school holidays I really 1) _____ to know them. They came to stay with us and we 2) _____ a lot of time together. We discovered that we 3) _____ a lot in common. They've had a 4) _____ time recently because their father lost his job. Fortunately, our parents get on 5) _____ each other and my mother advised Uncle George how to deal 6) _____ the situation. She told him to 7) _____ calm and not fall 8) _____ with the man he worked for.

1	A get	**(B)** got	C had	D have
2	A stay	B stayed	C spent	D spend
3	A have	B hold	C get	D got
4	A good	B worse	C fast	D hard
5	A to	B with	C at	D for
6	A for	B at	C with	D about
7	A hold	B have	C get	D stay
8	A out	B in	C off	D against

5 Complete the crossword with adjectives ending in -ed or -ing.

¹A	M	A	Z	²I	N	G

³E

⁴F

⁵B

⁶S

⁷A

⁸E

Across

1 It's _____ what you can do when you try!

3 We're all _____ about the concert!

6 The news about Oscar winning a prize was really _____. I didn't know he played chess so well.

7 I'm really _____ with Tom, he's upset me.

8 Holly heard what I said about her and I was really _____. My face went red!

Down

2 The programme about horses was very _____.

4 The horses were _____ by the loud noises.

5 I don't like this game, I think it's _____.

6 Choose the correct words.

1 It's *surprising/boring* how well Lily and Noah get on.

2 I'm *bored/amazed* with this game. Let's play something else.

3 There's no mobile phone signal here. It's really *annoying/exciting*.

4 Please don't shout in front of everyone in the café. It's very *embarrassing/surprising*.

5 I'm *annoyed/bored* that you didn't tell me you weren't coming!

6 There's no need to feel *amazed/embarrassed*. I understand how you feel.

7 Were you and Sophie *surprised/interested* to find out that you have something in common?

8 I don't want to spend time with Alfie and William. They're *amazing/boring*.

7 Complete the film review with one word in each space. The first letter has been given.

The boy from another world

Last night's film, *The boy from another world*, was very strange. At first, I thought the film was just another 1) b*oring* 'boy-meets-girl' story. A teenage girl is 2) e_____ when she meets a good-looking boy. She thinks he is 3) i_____ and she wants to get to know him better. She is 4) s_____ to discover that he isn't an ordinary teenager like everyone else. He comes from another planet and he has 5) a_____ powers. He understands people's thoughts and he is often 6) a_____ with them. When he gets angry, he does some terrible and 7) f_____ things. I have to say that I enjoyed the film. I'm 8) e_____ to admit it, but at the end, when the boy went home to his own world, I cried.

8 Complete the conversation. Use one adjective in each space.

James: I'm 1) _____bored_____ with staying in and watching TV. Let's go out.

Poppy: But this wildlife documentary is really 2) _____.

James: I didn't know you were 3) _____ in animals.

Poppy: Well, I think these snakes are 4) _____! They're beautiful and they move really fast.

James: I don't want to look. I'm 5) _____ of snakes.

Poppy: Sorry, I didn't know. I'll turn it off. Let's go out, then.

James: But now it's raining really hard. How 6) _____!

GRAMMAR

Talking about ability and possibility

1 Complete the sentences. Use *can* or *can't* and the verbs from the lists.

Charlotte's phone
- ✓ make calls
- ✓ send text messages
- ✗ take photos
- ✗ connect to the internet

Will's e-reader
- ✓ read books
- ✓ listen to stories
- ✗ make calls
- ✗ send text messages

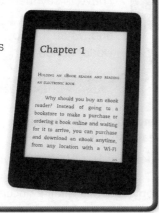

Chapter 1

HOLDING AN EBOOK READER AND READING AN ELECTRONIC BOOK

Why should you buy an eBook reader? Instead of going to a bookstore to make a purchase or ordering a book online and waiting for it to arrive, you can purchase and download an eBook anytime, from any location with a WI-FI

1 Charlotte *can make* calls with her phone.
2 She _____ text messages.
3 Charlotte _____ photos.
4 She _____ connect to the internet.
5 Will _____ books on his e-reader.
6 He _____ to stories.
7 Will _____ calls.
8 He _____ text messages.

2 Choose the correct words.

Training your dog
Do
- ■ keep your dog on a lead at first because it 1) *couldn't/might not* come when you call it.
- ■ give clear instructions. Then your dog 2) *will be able to/could* understand what you want.
- ■ keep training sessions short because your dog 3) *could/will be able to* become tired. A tired dog 4) *couldn't/won't be able to* concentrate.

Don't
- ■ let your dog take control, it 5) *could/will be able to* become dangerous.
- ■ encourage small children to play with your dog, it 6) *can/might* bite them and you 7) *will be able to/could* get into trouble.
- ■ shout at your dog. You 8) *might/will be able to* frighten it. When your dog doesn't do what you tell it, it 9) *might not/couldn't* understand what you want.

3 Complete the conversation with the best answer, A, B, C or D, for each space.

Daniel: What animals 1) _____ see at the zoo tomorrow?

Mum: We 2) _____ see lots of animals, but we'll have to choose because the zoo is very big and we 3) _____ to see everything.

Daniel: I want to see the monkeys, but they're very clever and I think they 4) _____ get out of their cages.

Mum: Don't worry. There are two doors to the cages, so that the keepers 5) _____ go inside to feed the monkeys. They lock the outside door so that the monkeys 6) _____ escape.

1 Ⓐ will we be able to   **B** could we
   C might we   **D** can't we
2 **A** can't   **B** will be able to
   C couldn't   **D** might not
3 **A** could   **B** will be able to
   C couldn't   **D** won't be able to
4 **A** won't be able to   **B** can't
   C might   **D** couldn't
5 **A** will be able to   **B** might
   C can't   **D** can
6 **A** couldn't   **B** can't
   C might   **D** might not

4 Complete the notice with *can/can't* or *will/won't be able to*.

Can you swim?

Yes: Take a life-saving certificate. Become a lifeguard. Get a holiday job at the pool. Have fun and earn money.

No: Take a beginner's course. Learn to swim in three weeks. Have fun playing water sports and games.

You 1) ___ *can* ___ already swim. You
2) _____ take our advanced course.
Get a life-saving certificate and qualify as a
lifeguard. After that you 3) _____ get a
summer job at the swimming pool. Then you
4) _____ have fun and earn money at
the same time.
You 5) _____ swim. Take our
beginner's course and you 6) _____
learn to swim in three weeks.
You 7) _____ get a job at the pool, but
you 8) _____ have fun playing water
sports and games.

Zero conditional, first conditional and *unless*

5 Match the sentence beginnings (1–6) with the endings (A–F).

1 If you have something in common with someone, _E_
2 If she apologises to me, _____
3 If you don't want to spend time with me, _____
4 If you can't deal with a problem, _____
5 If you stay calm, _____
6 If you want to get to know Ryan, _____

A please tell me.
B I'll introduce you.
C you'll be able to explain the problem.
D we won't fall out.
E you usually get on with them.
F ask a friend to help you.

6 Rewrite the sentences using *unless*.

1 Don't tell James if you don't want everyone to know.
Don't tell James unless you want everyone to know.
2 Don't wait for them if they don't call you.

3 Don't come to the cinema if you don't want to see the film.

4 Let's stop and have a coffee if you aren't too busy.

5 Let's watch the documentary if you haven't already seen it.

6 We could eat later if you aren't too hungry.

7 Choose the correct words.

1 If you *want/will want* to take a photo, *you press/ you'll press* this button.
2 *I send/I'll send* you an invitation if you *give/will give* me your mobile number.
3 My dog *never comes/will never come* unless *I give/I'll give* it a biscuit.
4 Your mother *is/will be* worried about you if you *don't call/won't call* her.
5 If Lily *concentrates/will concentrate*, *she always wins/she'll always win* the game.
6 If you *don't/won't* listen, you *don't/won't* know what to do.
7 You *don't/won't* get to know them unless you *talk/ will talk* to them.

8 Complete the conversation with the correct form of the verbs in brackets.

Lucas: Hi Dan. Listen, I'm on my way, but I'm late.
If I 1) ___ *miss* ___ (miss) the bus,
I 2) _____ (let) you know.
Dan: OK. I 3) _____ (not buy) the
train tickets unless I 4) _____
(know) you're coming. Send me a text if you
5) _____ (catch) the bus.
Lucas: If I 6) _____ (be) late, please
7) _____ (tell) Dylan I'm sorry.
Dan: OK, I'm sure he 8) _____
(understand) the situation if I
9) _____ (explain) it to him.

Revision Units 5 – 6

VOCABULARY

1 Find and write the sports words. There are four things to wear, two things to use and two places to do sports.

g	o	g	g	l	e	s	r	r
c	g	l	o	b	r	b	a	a
o	l	o	g	a	d	o	c	c
u	u	v	l	t	r	a	c	k
r	v	e	s	o	e	r	s	e
t	s	s	g	a	m	d	b	t
h	h	e	l	m	e	t	a	t
w	e	t	s	u	i	t	c	w
w	o	u	r	t	r	a	k	c

Things to wear
1 _____goggles_____
2 _____
3 _____
4 _____

Things to use
1 _____
2 _____

Places to do sports
1 _____
2 _____

2 Complete the sentences with these words.

> beats ~~hits~~ kicks match prizes
> races racket scores wins

Roger is a great tennis player. He 1) _____hits_____ the ball very hard with his 2) _____. He usually 3) _____ his opponent.

Ryan is a brilliant footballer. He 4) _____ a lot of goals. When he plays a 5) _____, he often 6) _____ the ball into the net.

Usain is a fantastic athlete. He 7) _____ a lot of 8) _____ because he runs 9) _____ very fast.

3 Choose the correct words.

Ask Aunt Lucy

Dear Aunt Lucy
I'm 1) _having/spending/being_ a hard time at school. It's difficult to 2) _do/get/stay_ calm and concentrate in class because I don't know how to 3) _solve/sort/deal_ with the problem. Some new boys joined our class and at first it was easy to 4) _fall/get/deal_ on with them. Now that I've 5) _got/had/come_ to know them better, I don't think we 6) _are/know/have_ anything in common. They are often unkind to other people in the class. I don't want to 7) _give/spend/use_ time with them now, but I don't want to 8) _get/fall/be_ out with them either because I think they'll be unkind to me.
Ava

4 Complete the sentences with the correct form of the words in brackets.

1 The most _____surprising_____ (surprise) thing about synchronised swimming is how hard it is!
2 I'm _____ (excite) about the final on Saturday.
3 Don't be _____ (embarrass) about not finishing the marathon. It's a very long race.
4 Cycling is an _____ (excite) sport. It's really fast.
5 I'm _____ (surprise) that you enjoy mud running. You don't like being cold and dirty.
6 Climbing may be fun to do, but it's _____ (bore) to watch!
7 Oscar was _____ (annoy) about losing the race.
8 I love kickboxing, it's an _____ (amaze) sport.

GRAMMAR

1 Complete the conversation with the present perfect form of the verbs in brackets.

George: Hi, William. 1) *Have you met* (you / meet) Charlotte? She 2) _____ (just / started) at our school. She 3) _____ (already / make) a lot of friends, but I 4) _____ (not introduce) her to everyone yet.

William: Hi there, Charlotte. I 5) _____ (already / discover) that we've got something in common! I 6) _____ (know) your cousin Sam for a long time! We 7) _____ (be) friends online since last year.

Charlotte: That's great! Sam 8) _____ (already / tell) me he had a friend at this school, so now I can tell him that I 9) _____ (just / meet) you!

2 Complete the text with the best answer, A, B, C or D, for each space.

Summer camp	⇦ ⇨
	Cancel Share Post

George and I 1) _____ friends for a long time. We 2) _____ at summer camp five years ago and we 3) _____ on well. We 4) _____ a lot of time together since we 5) _____ , but last year we 6) _____ each other at all. We 7) _____ out and George 8) _____ meeting next month. We 9) _____ to go to another summer camp next year, but we 10) _____ where we'll go yet.

Support

1 **A** were   **B** have been
  C has been   **D** was
2 **A** met   **B** have met
  C has met   **D** meet
3 **A** has got   **B** have got
  C got   **D** get
4 **A** have spent   **B** spend
  C spent   **D** has spent
5 **A** have met   **B** has met
  C met   **D** meet
6 **A** haven't seen   **B** hasn't seen
  C don't see   **D** didn't see

7 **A** hasn't fallen   **B** haven't fallen
  C don't fall   **D** didn't fall
8 **A** have just suggested **B** has just suggested
  C just suggested   **D** just suggests
9 **A** already plan   **B** has already planned
  C have already planned **D** planned
10 **A** don't decide   **B** hasn't decided
   C didn't decide   **D** haven't decided

3 Choose the correct words.

It's surprising what you 1) *can/could/might* do when you try. You decide to take up running and you imagine that you 2) *can/might/will be able to* compete in a marathon very soon. Then you start training and find you 3) *couldn't/can't/won't be able to* run very fast and you 4) *can't/couldn't/won't be able to* run very far. You don't give up and after a few training sessions you find that you 5) *might/could/can* run faster than you managed at first. You think you 6) *might/can/won't be able to* enter for a marathon next year. You hope to complete the course. You know you 7) *might/can't/won't be able to* beat the really fast runners, but you 8) *might/can/won't be able to* beat some people.

4 Complete the text with the correct form of the verbs in brackets.

When people 1) *watch* (watch) sporting events on TV, they often 2) _____ (start) training. If TV 3) _____ (not show) women's sports or Paralympic events, people 4) _____ (not know) about them. Sports 5) _____ (not become) popular unless they 6) _____ (be) on TV. We know that more people 7) _____ (take up) cycling if a popular sports person like Bradley Wiggins 8) _____ (win) the Tour de France.

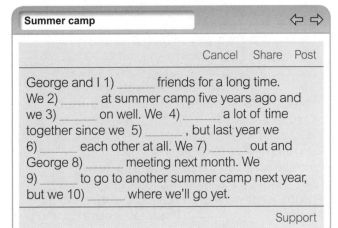

33

That's entertainment

VOCABULARY

1 Find and write seven entertainment words.

c	e	c	r	c	c	u	e	r
h	s	r	d	r	o	w	r	i
o	r	c	h	e	s	t	r	a
i	o	o	g	x	t	c	d	i
r	o	a	c	i	u	r	a	o
a	t	e	h	t	m	e	s	g
s	m	e	e	u	e	c	a	c
a	u	d	i	e	n	c	e	i
t	r	e	e	e	c	a	t	e

1 _____*row*_____   5 _____
2 _____   6 _____
3 _____   7 _____
4 _____

2 Complete the entertainment words with *a, e, i, o* or *u*.

1 r_o_w
2 ch____r
3 c__st__m__
4 __x__t
5 ____d____nc__
6 ____rch____str__
7 st__g__

3 Write the words in Exercise 2 under the correct headings.

People	Places	Things
	row	

4 Complete the sentences with entertainment words. The first letter has been given.

1 When the show finished the a*udience* stood up and left the theatre.
2 You can't sit in that r_____. It's for the photographers.
3 Emily plays the trumpet in the school o_____ .
4 The actor came on the s_____ and started talking.
5 I'd love to sing in a c_____, but my voice is terrible.
6 We tried to leave the concert, but we couldn't find the e_____ .
7 She didn't like her c_____ because it was too long to walk in.

5 Complete the blog. Use one word in each space.

> **goodtheatreblog.com** ⇦ ⇨
>
> 💬 View previous comments   Cancel   Share   Post
>
> My local theatre is only small, but it's got
> 1) _____*rows*_____ of comfortable, red seats that are great for relaxing and enjoying shows. Tonight the 2) _____ was full of students who came to watch a musical by the Creative Teens Theatre Company. A live 3) _____ played music during the show and a 4) _____ sang an unusual mixture of classical and pop music. When the show finished the performers came back on 5) _____ and continued for another half hour. Everything was great about the show except for the 6) _____. The actors looked hot and uncomfortable all night.
>
> Write a comment   Support

6 Match the photos (A–F) with the sentences (1–6). Use the words in bold to help you.

A

B

C

D

E

F

1 They're going to **film** a documentary about the town. _E_

2 In today's programme we're **interviewing** a local pop star. ......

3 Amelia is **recording** an album of her own songs. ......

4 Everybody enjoyed **performing** in the school play. ......

5 I'm **reviewing** a film for my English homework. ......

6 The audience **clapped** for ages and finally the actors came back on stage. ......

7 Choose the correct words.

1 We're excited that they're *performing/filming* our school for the programme. We're going to be on TV!

2 Guess what? I'm *interviewing/recording* the pop group *Flippers* for the school magazine.

3 Before the show a comedian came on stage and *filmed/entertained* the audience with a few jokes.

4 If you like the cinema and writing, you could *book/review* films for a magazine.

8 Complete the text with the best answer, A, B, C or D, for each space.

This week, *Entertainment News* is 1) .... *The Voice* - Saturday night's new talent show to find Britain's best singer.

It's a simple idea. The contestant comes onto the 2) .... and gives a short introduction. Then the studio 3) .... watches as he or she sings in front of four judges. The judges can't see who is 4) .... to them because they have their backs to the singer. If they like the singer, they press a red light and their chair turns around. When this happens everybody starts 5) .... because it means the singer is good. When more than one professional turns around, the contestant chooses which one he or she wants to work with.

The winner of the competition has the chance to 6) .... an album. The professionals are good fun and know how to 7) .... the audience with stories of how they became famous.

If you'd like to be in the studio audience, call now to 8) .... tickets - they're free!

1 A filming   B recording
   C reviewing   D interviewing

2 A row   B stage
   C exit   D orchestra

3 A audience   B choir
   C orchestra   D costume

4 A performing   B entertaining
   C acting   D recording

5 A filming   B interviewing
   C booking   D clapping

6 A book   B perform
   C entertain   D record

7 A interview   B review
   C entertain   D perform

8 A record   B book
   C film   D review

GRAMMAR

Second conditional

1 Match the sentence beginnings (1–7) with the endings (A–G).

1 If I won two tickets to the festival, _F_
2 If the school had a good choir, ...
3 The theatre would lose money ....
4 If I didn't like the show, ...
5 She would learn faster ....
6 If the stage were bigger, ...
7 We wouldn't stay late at the concert ....

A I would leave early.
B if we had school the next day.
C if she practised more.
D the dancers would have more space.
E if the tickets were too cheap.
F I would ask you to come with me.
G I would sing in it.

2 Choose the correct words.

1 If I *am/were* you, I would join the school drama club.
2 If you *interview/interviewed* a famous person, what would you ask?
3 I wouldn't stay at the concert if I *don't like/ didn't like* the music.
4 What would you do if you *lost/lose* your iPod?
5 If we *have/had* more music lessons at school, I'd be really happy.
6 Emily would call us if she *wanted/wants* to see us.
7 What would Liam do if he *isn't/wasn't* a pop singer?
8 I wouldn't wear that costume on stage if I *were/am* you.

3 Complete the second conditional sentences. Use the correct form of the verbs in brackets.

1 If we asked them, _would they sing_ (sing) for us?
2 I _____ (not play) the drums in here if I were you.
3 Jake and Olivia _____ (go) to the concert if they had tickets.
4 If you liked the music, _____ (dance) with me?
5 You _____ (love) this festival if you were here.
6 The audience _____ (not clap) if they weren't happy with the show.
7 _____ (you / travel) around the world if you were in a pop group?
8 If you passed the exam, you _____ (get) a place in a good music school.

4 Complete the magazine interview with the correct form of the verbs in brackets.

Every week at *Pop News* we invite our readers to ask their favourite celebrity the question 'What would you do if ...?' This week we say 'Hi' to Billy from the band IDX.

Hi, Billy, what would you do if you 1) _weren't_ **(not be) in a pop group?**

Ah, a difficult question! If I 2) _____ (not sing), I'd be really bored. Singing is my passion.

If you won the lottery, what 3) _____ **(you / buy)?**

Great question. If I 4) _____ (have) lots of money, I'd buy a big house for my family.

Billy, if you 5) _____ **(buy) a pet, what would it be?**

Well, I've already got two dogs, but if I bought another pet, it 6) _____ (be) a snake.

What would you do if you 7) _____ **(be) ill on the night of a concert?**

I'm never ill, but if I was really bad, I 8) _____ (call) the doctor.

And finally, you hate flying, Billy. What would you do if the band 9) _____ **(want) to do a concert in another country.**

Well, if it wasn't too far, I 10) _____ (travel) by train. I love trains.

5 Complete the second sentence so that it means the same as the first.

1 We can't go to the concert because we haven't got tickets.

If we _____ *had* _____ tickets, we could go to the concert.

2 I'd speak to Anna, but she isn't at home.

If Anna _____ at home, I would speak to her.

3 I don't dance when the music isn't very good.

I _____ if the music was better.

4 The theatre is closing because it doesn't make enough money.

If the theatre _____ more money, it wouldn't close.

5 She isn't in the choir because she hasn't got enough time.

If she had more time, she _____ in the choir.

6 We don't practise in this room because it's too small.

If this room was bigger, we _____ in it.

Subject questions and object questions

6 Read the sentences, then choose the correct words in the questions.

1 Rita Ora wrote that song.

What/Who wrote that song?

2 The ticket fell on the floor.

What/Who fell on the floor?

3 The choir came onto the stage.

What/Who came onto the stage?

4 The costumes were fantastic.

What/Who were fantastic?

5 The exit was difficult to find.

What/Who was difficult to find?

6 The bad weather ruined the festival.

What/Who ruined the festival?

7 Complete the questions with *do*, *does*, *did* or –.

1 What _____ *did* _____ you record last month?

2 Who _____ – _____ interviewed you for the magazine?

3 What _____ happened at the festival?

4 Who _____ she usually sing with on stage?

5 What _____ they see at the theatre last night?

6 What _____ helps them relax before a concert?

7 What _____ they want to do today?

8 Who _____ plays an instrument?

8 Make questions for these answers.

1 who / teach / you / play the guitar / ?

Q: _____ *Who taught you to play the guitar?*

A: My dad taught me to play the guitar.

2 what / your friends / think about your music / ?

Q: _____

A: My friends think my music's great.

3 who / write / your songs / ?

Q: _____

A: I write all of them.

4 what / be / the first song / you wrote / ?

Q: _____

A: The first song that I wrote was 'Thunder'.

5 who / you / listen to / when you were at school / ?

Q: _____

A: I listened to Jay'z ... all the time.

6 what / you / buy / with the money from your first album / ?

Q: _____

A: I bought a new guitar!

7 what / make / you special / ?

Q: _____

A: My music makes me special. It's different.

Going away

VOCABULARY

1 **Choose the correct definition, A or B.**

1 destination
   A The place that you come from.
   B The place that you are travelling to.

2 flight
   A A journey by plane.
   B A journey by ferry.

3 border
   A The line that separates two countries.
   B The land next to the sea.

4 motorway
   A A narrow road in the countryside.
   B A wide road for driving fast over long distances.

5 passport
   A A small official book with your photo that you use to travel abroad.
   B A piece of paper that you buy to travel somewhere or to go to an event.

6 sightseeing
   A Visiting famous or interesting places.
   B Buying things, usually in shops.

7 traffic jam
   A A large space where people leave cars.
   B A long line of cars on the road, often moving very slowly.

2 **Complete the sentences with travel words. The first letter has been given.**

1 She didn't enjoy the f*light* to New York because the plane was hot and noisy.

2 This snow is going to d_____ the bus and we'll arrive late.

3 The j_____ home took eight hours and it was very boring.

4 The planes can't l_____ on this island because there are too many mountains.

5 We're going on a t_____ to Disneyland. I can't wait!

6 Will and his friends are going to t_____ around Europe by train this summer.

3 **Choose the correct words.**

1 They had a four-hour *delay*/*flight* before the plane finally left.

2 The train crosses the *abroad*/*border* between Germany and Poland.

3 We heard about the *traffic jam*/*destination* on the news so we left early.

4 Jack's gone *abroad*/*sightseeing* for the first time. He's never left his country before.

5 The plane can't *land*/*take off* until the pilot arrives.

6 The history class is going on a *trip*/*journey* to a castle today.

4 **Match the photos (A–F) with the messages (1–6).**

1 Guess who's forgotten their passport? _C_

2 We can't check in until 10 pm #alongwait _____

3 I've been in a traffic jam for three hours ☹ _____

4 The plane's going to take off soon. _____

5 We're finally leaving the motorway #goinghome _____

6 His plane lands in ten minutes. _____

5 Read the sentences. Decide if the underlined <u>word</u> is a noun (n) or a verb (v).

1 It took us a long time to <u>check in</u> our bags because the airport was very busy. *v*

2 I don't think the plane can <u>land</u> in this weather. ....

3 I was frightened during the <u>take-off</u> because the plane made a loud noise. ....

4 Emily met some friends on the train <u>journey</u>. ....

5 One day I want to <u>travel</u> around the world. ....

6 After a long <u>delay</u> they finally announced our flight. ....

6 Choose the best answer, A, B or C.

1 A lot of people are waiting to .... their bags at the airport.
   A delay
   B check in
   C take off

2 During the two-hour .... we watched a film.
   A flight
   B border
   C motorway

3 Oliver heard about the .... so decided to go by bike.
   A border
   B motorway
   C traffic jam

4 Today the students are .... in London, but tomorrow they begin their classes.
   A travelling
   B abroad
   C sightseeing

5 Alice enjoyed her holiday in Brazil, but she's very tired after the long .... home.
   A journey
   B trip
   C travel

6 I'm always very nervous during the ...., but when the plane is in the air, I'm fine.
   A delay
   B take-off
   C check-in

7 Complete the email with these words.

abroad flights journey motorway
passport sightseeing travel ~~trip~~

mailbox Today | Mail | Calendar | Contacts

Reply | Reply All | Forward | Delete

From: **Daniel** Subject: **School trip**

Hi Maria
Guess what? I'm going on a school 1) ___trip___ to Istanbul. I've already started planning what I need for the long 2) .... We're going to 3) .... by coach because the 4) .... are very expensive. It's going to take 36 hours! I don't know how much I will see because we'll be on the boring 5) .... most of the time. I've just found my 6) .... with a very embarrassing photograph in it. This will be my first holiday 7) .... because we usually go camping in the mountains near where we live. I can't wait to go 8) .... and want to visit the Topkapi Palace. I'll send you some photos.
Bye for now
Daniel

8 Put the letters in the correct order to make travel words. Find the hidden message.

1 n a l d | l | a | n | d | (4)

2 e a d y l | | | | | (3)

3 d a b o r a | | | | | | | (10) (8)

4 n y u r e j o | | | | | | | (6)

5 r o t s a p s p | | | | | | | | (12) (7)

6 h i e t n g e s g i s | | | | | | | | | | | (11) (1) (9) (5)

7 s i t n i t e n a d o | | | | | | | | | | |

		V									
1	2	3	4	5	6	7	8	9	10	11	12

GRAMMAR

Defining relative clauses

1 **Put the words in the correct order to make sentences.**

1 is / the / that / bag / I / yesterday / bought / This / .
   This is the bag that I bought yesterday.

2 Emma / looking for / flight / a / that / in / stops / is / Paris / .

3 staying / my / with / live / cousins / Canada /who / in /We're / .

4 The / that / very / know / are / students / funny / we / .

5 That's / won / competition / boy / who / the / the / .

6 is / friend / visiting / a / he / who / on holiday / met / Liam / .

2 **Add *who* or *which/that* to complete the sentences where necessary.**

1 I've got a new rucksack ___*which*___ is perfect for camping.

2 Anna enjoyed the trip ___ her friends organised for her birthday.

3 There's a boy in my class ___ speaks five languages.

4 The sightseeing trip ___ we booked was brilliant.

5 I live in a town ___ is near the border with Poland.

6 Max can't find the photo ___ he needs for his passport.

7 I get on well with my brothers ___ also love travelling.

8 I know somebody ___ always arrives late.

3 **Choose the correct words.**

1 Do you remember the girl _who/which_ sat next to us on the plane?

2 The city _who/that_ I want to visit is Buenos Aires.

3 We're travelling on the train _who/which_ goes to Dublin.

4 The people _who/which_ work here are very friendly.

5 Where are the tickets _who/which_ I gave you this morning?

6 There was a long delay at the airport _who/that_ made people angry.

4 **Read the sentences. Decide if *who/which/that* refers to the object (O) or the subject (S).**

1 We were in a traffic jam *that* lasted five hours.   _S_

2 The motorway *which* they used was very busy.   _O_

3 That's my neighbour *who* works at the airport.   ___

4 I've got a friend *who* has won a holiday in New York.   ___

5 What's the name of the website *that* I can use to buy a cheap flight?   ___

6 The teachers are planning a trip *which* the students will love.   ___

7 The man *who* looked at my passport laughed at the photo.   ___

8 The tourists *that* we saw at the check-in were very impatient.   ___

5 **Complete the blog with *who*, *which*, *that* or – . Sometimes more than one answer is possible.**

holidayblog.com

View previous comments   Cancel   Share   Post

Do you want a holiday 1) _which/that_ offers you something different and exciting? You should go on an International Summer Camp! I tried one last year and had a holiday 2) ___ I will never forget. Now I've got friends 3) ___ come from all around the world. Each day you do different activities 4) ___ you choose from an amazing programme. You learn with teachers 5) ___ are experts in their activity. I tried activities 6) ___ were completely new for me, like sky-diving and film-making. At first I was very nervous, but I soon found friends 7) ___ were doing the same activities. The weekends were more relaxing, with sightseeing and shopping trips. One day we met some friends in the town 8) ___ invited us to their party. It was brilliant!

Write a comment   Support

must, have to

6 Match the sentences (1–6) with the sentences (A–F).

1 You must get a passport. _C_
2 There's a lot of snow on the road. ......
3 We don't have to go sightseeing now. ......
4 They have to go now. ......
5 Jake will be late because of the traffic jam. ......
6 You mustn't leave your bag there. ......

A Somebody might take it.
B We must drive slowly.
C You can't travel abroad without it.
D We have to start without him.
E The train leaves in ten minutes.
F Everything is open tomorrow.

7 Complete the sentences with these verbs.

> didn't have to   ~~don't have to~~   had to
> 'll have to   must   mustn't

1 You _don't have to_ buy the tickets online, but they're cheaper.
2 The train stopped at the border because we .... show our passports.
3 I .... see the doctor. I've had a headache for two days.
4 We .... be late. The bus will leave without us.
5 Alice .... travel on her own. She met an old friend on the train.
6 The flight leaves tomorrow at 6 a.m. We .... get up very early.

8 Complete the conversation with the best answer, A, B or C, for each space.

José: Hi Maria, are you ready for your holiday?
Maria: No, not at all. My passport's only just arrived. I 1) .... get a new one because I lost my old one.
José: That's typical of you, Maria. When do you 2) .... leave?
Maria: We're flying at seven o'clock in the morning so we 3) .... be at the airport by five o'clock. Dad says we 4) .... leave the house early in case there's a traffic jam.
José: But you hate getting up early!
Maria: I know. I 5) .... forget to set my alarm. Anyway, I'm going to pack my bags and then I'm going to bed.
José: That's a pity. I'm just going to Anna's party.
Maria: Anna's party? Hang on, let me think. I 6) .... pack now.
José: Yes, you do Maria. You can go to the party, but you 7) .... pack first. I'll come and help. We 8) .... be there until nine o'clock.
Maria: Brilliant. I hate packing, but I'll do it faster if you help me.

1 A 'll have to
  (B) had to
  C must
2 A have to
  B must
  C will have to
3 A had to
  B don't have to
  C 'll have to
4 A mustn't
  B had to
  C must
5 A don't have to
  B mustn't
  C must
6 A didn't have to
  B don't have to
  C must
7 A had to
  B have to
  C don't have to
8 A mustn't
  B didn't have to
  C don't have to

Revision Units 7 – 8

VOCABULARY

1 Complete the crossword.

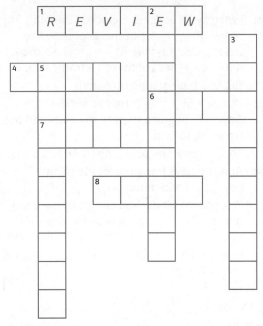

Across

1 Write a report about a new film, book, etc.
4 Arrange to have or do something at a particular time
6 The way out of a place
7 A group of people who sing together
8 Hit your hands together to show that you enjoyed something

Down

2 Do something that other people like watching or listening to
3 Ask someone questions
5 A group of people who play instruments together

2 Choose the best answer, A, B or C.

1 We tried to _____ a seat for the theatre, but there weren't any left.
   A perform   **B** book   C review
2 Emma's rock band is going to _____ an album this summer.
   A entertain   B film   C record
3 I always sit near the front _____ at the theatre so that I can see everything.
   A stage   B row   C exit
4 I've got to _____ this book for my English class, but I haven't read it yet.
   A review   B perform   C interview
5 Jake's left the _____ because he doesn't want to play the violin any more.
   A choir   B orchestra   C stage
6 This is the same _____ that I wore for the school play last year.
   A stage   B audience   C costume

3 Complete the sentences with these words.

> check-in   delay   flight   journey   ~~sightseeing~~   take-off   traffic jam

1 You need at least a week for _sightseeing_ in New York because there are so many interesting places to visit.
2 It was a very boring car _____ so my brother and I started to play silly games.
3 If there's a _____ with our train we'll have time to go to the café for lunch.
4 Nick arrived late at the airport and the _____ desk was closed.
5 We didn't enjoy the _____ because it was a small plane and the seats weren't comfortable.
6 Let's walk home. There's a long _____ in the centre of town and it will be quicker than going by bus.
7 I like the _____ best, especially when the plane climbs above the clouds.

4 **Complete the diary entry with the correct words. The first letter has been given.**

Thursday

My new 1) p*assport* finally arrived with its silly photo and now I'm getting ready for my first holiday 2) a_____ . I'm going to Carcassonne in the south of France. The town is near the 3) b_____ with Spain so I hope to practise my French and Spanish. We've got a 4) f_____ to Toulouse, but then we have to travel by car to Carcassonne. Mum says it will be a quick 5) j_____ because the 6) m_____ are very good in France. We've got to 7) c_____ for the flight at 3.45 a.m. so I have to start packing now. I can't wait. This time tomorrow I will be 8) s_____ in Carcassonne. There are lots of exciting places to visit, including a very old castle.

GRAMMAR

1 **Complete the conversation with the correct form of the verbs in brackets.**

Ben: If somebody 1) _*bought*_ (buy) you a holiday anywhere in the world, where _would you go_ (you / go), Amelia?

Amelia: I'd go to New York. If I 2) _____ (be) there in winter, I _____ (stay) near Central Park.

Ben: Yes, and you could go ice-skating.

Amelia: Exactly! I 3) _____ (not like) it if I _____ (be) on my own.

Ben: If you 4) _____ (can) take a friend, who _____ (it / be)?

Amelia: Phoebe. If she 5) _____ (come) too, we _____ (have) great fun.

Ben: 6) _____ (you / go) shopping if you _____ (be) in New York?

Amelia: Maybe. If we 7) _____ (have) lots of money, we _____ (book) tickets for the theatre every night.

2 **Choose the correct words.**

1 *Who/What* caused the delay at the airport?
2 *Who/What* did you interview last night?
3 *Who/What* found your passport?
4 *Who/What* was the play about?
5 *Who/What* did the choir sing?
6 *Who/What* was at the check-in desk?
7 *Who/What* bought the tickets?
8 *Who/What* happened on the motorway?

3 **Join the sentences. Use *who*, *that* or *which*. Sometimes more than one answer is possible.**

1 I enjoyed the play. We saw it at the theatre.
   I enjoyed the play that/which we saw at the theatre.

2 These are the tickets. They cost £20.
   _____

3 I've got a friend. She wants to be a pilot.
   _____

4 I liked the actor. He was wearing a gold costume.
   _____

5 Have you seen the passport? It arrived today.
   _____

6 That's the girl. She was ill on the flight.
   _____

4 **Complete the letter with these verbs.**

didn't have to   don't have to   had to
~~must~~   mustn't   will have to

Mill Bank School

Dear parents and students,

School trip to the Edinburgh Festival

All students 1) _*must*_ be at the school at 7.30 a.m. This is important because the coach leaves at 8 o'clock. Last year some students arrived late and 2) _____ travel by train.

Please remember that students 3) _____ eat on the coach. However, the coach will stop on the motorway so that students can have lunch.

The coach will park near the festival site. At the end of the festival, students 4) _____ return to the car park.

Students 5) _____ take bags or coats to the festival. They can leave them on the coach.

Please bring a passport or a student identity card. Students 6) _____ show them last year, but it's a good idea to take them.

We hope everybody has a great day.

Mr Hiller
Head Teacher

43

09 Weird and wonderful world

VOCABULARY

1 Match the words (1–7) with the words (a–g) to make hobbies and interests.

1	collecting	a	a musical instrument
2	doing	b	drama
3	keeping	c	fit
4	making	d	gaming
5	making	e	jewellery
6	online	f	key rings
7	practising	g	models

2 Write the names of the hobbies.

1 *cooking*

2 _____

3 _____

4 _____

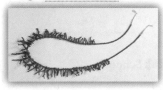

5 _____

6 _____

3 Choose the correct words.

1 The only problem with my new camera is the *screen/battery*. It doesn't last long.

2 Jack's gone to buy a new *paintbrush/glue*. He's got an Art exam tomorrow.

3 I've broken a cup. Perhaps I can repair it with some *glue/pastry*.

4 Amelia went to buy the *ingredients/recipe* for a chocolate cake, but she forgot the flour.

5 I didn't use the *zoom lens/screen* for this photo so you can't really see people's faces.

6 Have you got any *ingredients/scissors*? I want to cut this funny picture out of the magazine.

4 Complete the sentences with these words and phrases.

> chill out   ~~keeping fit~~   hang out with
> ingredients   join in   taking photos

1 Liam and his brother are into _*keeping fit*_ . They both want to teach sport one day.

2 I didn't feel well on the school trip and couldn't _____ the fun.

3 We haven't got the right _____ to make a salad. I'll have to go shopping.

4 In the school holidays I usually _____ other friends who make models.

5 The girls are mad about _____ . They never go out without their cameras.

6 You look very tired. You should _____ at home before you go to piano practice.

5 Find eight hobby words. Write them under the correct heading.

i	d	n	h	r	p	g	e	e	s	h
n	r	r	s	s	a	t	l	p	s	i
g	n	e	a	i	c	c	t	u	e	c
r	b	c	c	s	s	r	r	p	e	o
e	e	i	h	i	b	b	a	h	i	r
d	s	p	a	s	t	r	y	r	n	o
i	s	e	s	n	s	r	r	e	s	y
e	e	t	i	a	o	t	e	n	o	d
n	b	a	t	t	e	r	y	t	e	p
t	p	i	c	e	c	c	e	c	i	r
s	c	i	s	s	o	r	s	t	r	s

Cooking	Making models	Photography
ingredients		

6 **Write the letters in the correct order to make hobby words and complete the sentences.**

1 If you have a computer, *online gaming* (elionn mggnia) is brilliant and you can play with all your friends.

2 Have you got anything that I can use to clean the dirty _____ (enrsec) on this camera?

3 Nathan enjoys _____ (onicokg), but he's really bad at it. That cake was terrible.

4 Max wants to _____ (onij ni) the dancing, but he's too embarrassed.

5 The students always enjoy _____ (igdno aardm) after school and there are some great actors in the group.

6 I need some strong _____ (egul) so that I can repair my skateboard.

7 **Complete the email with these words and phrases.**

are mad about ~~chill out~~ hang out with
join in the fun keeping fit 'm into
online gaming

Subject: **How was your weekend?** ⇐ ⇒ ⌂

Hi Kieran
How was your weekend? Did you 1) *chill out* after your exam on Friday? I went to the beach. Some of my friends 2) _____ taking photos, so we took some cool pictures of the beach in winter. On Saturday it rained all day, but my cousins were here. We all enjoy 3) _____ so we spent a lot of time on the computer. My little sister wanted to 4) _____ , but she was really annoying! I was glad it was sunny yesterday because I 5) _____ skateboarding at the moment and I wanted to go to the new skateboarding park. It's a great place to 6) _____ other skateboarders and I've made lots of friends. 7) _____ is really important and I think skateboarding is a good way to get exercise. Let's go together soon.
Bye for now
Laura

8 **Complete the class survey about students' hobbies. Use one or two words in each space.**

How do you spend your free time? We've found out some exciting facts about your hobbies and interests. Read the results of our class survey of 15 students.

5 people in the class have never tried 1) *making models* as a hobby and think that sticking things together with 2) _____ and then painting them can be boring. The rest said they enjoy it and have created robots, aeroplanes and mini animals.

6 people in the class regularly 3) _____ a musical instrument and **3** of them play the electric guitar. The other students in the class would like to buy one, but think they are too expensive.

10 students say that they are 4) _____ taking photos, especially with their mobile phones. Only **4** students prefer to use a real camera. **1** student has just bought a 5) _____ because she enjoys taking close up photos of the fish that she keeps at home.

8 students enjoy 6) _____ unusual things, from old keys to stamps from around the world and even old shoes!

The two most popular hobbies are 7) _____ (if somebody else buys the ingredients!) and 8) _____ , although it's only fun if you've got a good computer and your friends are playing.

The most popular way to spend your free time is with friends. **15** out of **15** students agree that hanging 9) _____ friends after school is the best way to have fun.

GRAMMAR

Reported statements

1 **Put the words in the correct order to make sentences.**

1 said / Luke / that / the / delicious / cake / was / .

Luke said that the cake was delicious.

2 would / said / beach / that / They / be / at / they / the / .

3 bored / girls / they / that / were / The / said / .

4 We / that / we / make / would / a / said / cake / .

5 fit / You / me / you / that / told / keeping / loved / .

6 her / Emma / the / sister / she / couldn't / that / use / camera / told / .

2 **Read the first sentence. Choose the correct words in the reported sentences.**

1 'I love making models.'
Nathan *said/told* that he loved making models.

2 'I can't find a recipe for the pizza.'
Olivia said that she *could/couldn't* find a recipe for the pizza.

3 'I don't want to do drama.'
Will said that he *didn't want/wanted* to do drama.

4 'I can't go to your party, Kate.'
I *said/told* Kate that I couldn't go to her party.

5 'I'll make some jewellery for you.'
Anna told me that she would make some jewellery for *I/me*.

6 'We often take photos of our friends.'
They said that they often took photos of *our/their* friends.

7 'We'll practise the piano later.'
They said that they *would/wouldn't* practise the piano later.

8 'Online gaming with friends is fun.'
She *said/told* me that online gaming with friends was fun.

3 **Complete the sentences with the correct form of *say* or *tell*.**

1 We ____told____ him that his model would win the competition.

2 Isaac _____ that he practised the guitar every day.

3 They _____ they would arrive at eight o'clock.

4 Sophie _____ her friends she would be late.

5 I _____ that I didn't want a party.

6 You _____ me you could do it.

4 **Complete the diary entries with these words.**

> him   me   played   said   ~~told~~
> wanted   would

Monday
Parents' evening at school! Mum and Dad have just got back. My music teacher 1) ____told____ my dad that I 2) _____ the guitar really well. Dad 3) _____ that he was really surprised because he and Mum can't play any instruments. Then Dad said that he 4) _____ get me a new guitar. Brilliant.

Tuesday
I told 5) _____ that I could help pay for the guitar, but he said that Granddad 6) _____ to pay for it. 'Why?' I asked. Then he told 7) _____ that Granddad learned to play the classical guitar when he was at school. However, when he was young he never had enough money for a good guitar.

5 **Complete the conversation with the correct past form of the verb in brackets.**

Nia: Hi Dan. Are you coming to drama class tonight?

Dan: No, I can't. I told my brother Tom I
1) _____would_____ (will) go swimming with him.

Nia: But, Dan, the drama teacher said we
2) _____ (have to) be at the last class. Don't you remember? She told us that we 3) _____ (need) to practise the songs together.

Dan: I know, but my parents are working. I told them it 4) _____ (be) my last drama class, but they said that they 5) _____ (not want) Tom to be on his own.

Nia: Oh, that's difficult, but I think I can help. My brother said he 6) _____ (want) to watch basketball on TV tonight. Perhaps you could leave Tom at my house?

Dan: That's a great idea. He told me they
7) _____ (like) the same team.

Nia: No problem, Dan. I said that I 8) _____ (can) help!

6 **Complete the reported sentences.**

> I'll send you the photos.

1 Harry said that he _would send me_ the photos.

> We can leave.

2 Emma told her friends that _____ leave.

> I'm tired.

3 Dan said that _____ tired.

> We don't have the right ingredients.

4 They said that _____ the right ingredients.

> Our models aren't very good.

5 They said that _____ very good.

> I'll call you later.

6 Alice told me that she _____ later.

used to

7 **Match the sentence beginnings (1–6) with the endings (A–F).**

1 I used to collect stamps, _C_

2 Did you use to do _____

3 Jessica didn't use to like dancing, _____

4 Did they use to watch _____

5 When you were young, did you use to _____

6 Jack didn't use to do sport, _____

A but she loves it now.

B black and white films on TV?

C but I'm interested in other things now.

D but now he plays tennis every day.

E drama after school?

F collect old keys?

8 **Complete the sentences. Use the correct form of *used to* and the verb in brackets.**

1 She _____used to enjoy_____ (enjoy) keeping fit.

2 Did Max _____ (paint) his models?

3 They _____ (not read) comics.

4 Jessica _____ (write) her own songs.

5 I _____ (not wear) any jewellery.

6 Did they _____ (keep) bees in their garden?

9 **Complete the interview. Use the correct form of *used to* and the verb in brackets.**

Interviewer: Welcome, Michel. It's great to meet a famous chef. Tell us, 1) _did you use to cook_ (you / cook) when you were young?

Michel: Yes, I did. Every summer I 2) _____ (help) my aunt in her hotel. It was only a small hotel, but she 3) _____ (do) all the cooking.

Interviewer: So, did she teach you to cook?

Michel: No, she 4) _____ (not have) much time, but I watched her and that's how I learned.

Interviewer: 5) _____ (you / dream) of becoming a famous chef?

Michel: Not at all! I always wanted to be a famous singer!

Interviewer: A singer?

Michel: Yes, I loved singing in the kitchen of the hotel, but everybody 6) _____ (tell) me to be quiet. I was terrible!

VOCABULARY

1 Match 1–8 with a–h to make skills for work phrases.

1	enjoy	**a**	new skills quickly
2	always do	**b**	my/your/his/her/their mind
3	stay	**c**	a challenge
4	make	**d**	my/your/his/her/their best
5	run	**e**	money
6	pick up	**f**	good team player
7	speak	**g**	a business
8	be a	**h**	calm under pressure

2 Put the words in the correct order to make sentences.

1 always / She / challenge / enjoys / a / .
   She always enjoys a challenge.

2 important / Making / is / James / money / very / to / .

3 often / They / speak / work / their / at / mind / .

4 good / skills / picking up / at / new / quickly / I'm / .

5 must / your / always / do / best / You / .

6 Dan / run / his / business / sister / a / and / fashion / .

7 you / to / want / be / Do / creative / ?

8 calm / It's / pressure / to / stay / under / difficult / .

3 Choose the correct words.

1 Nathan's doing a course in costume design. He loves being *a good team player/creative*.

2 The course is difficult at the moment, but I *enjoy a challenge/make money* and I'm learning quickly.

3 The hotel is very busy and guests can sometimes be difficult. It's important that you *work on your own/stay calm under pressure*.

4 This summer I'm helping on my uncle's farm. I won't *speak my mind/make money*, but it'll be fun.

5 The problem with Emma is that she always *speaks her mind/does her best*, but sometimes she says too much.

6 In the future I'd like to *work on my own/run a business* with some friends.

4 Complete the advert with the correct words.

CUP CAKE CAFÉ

Cup Cake Café is looking for someone special to join their busy team.

- Are you a good 1) ___team___ player?
- Do you 2) _____ a challenge?
- Can you 3) _____ under pressure?
- Do you always try to 4) _____ your best?
- Would you like to learn how to 5) _____ creative?

If you answered 'yes' to all the above questions, call us now.

Don't worry if you don't have the right experience.

Our friendly team will help you to 6) _____ new skills quickly.

5 Complete the words to make eight more negative adjectives.

¹I	P		I		N			
	²N		O	M			T	
		³I		P		S		B	E
	⁴		N		O		R		C
⁵U		S			L			
⁶N		X		E		I		E
		⁷		T			Y	
⁸U		F	R		E		D	L

6 Complete the sentences with the correct adjectives. The prefixes have been given.

1 Your essay is in*complete*. You've got to finish it before you email it to the teacher.

2 Can you take all your books and bags to your room? This lounge is so un_____ .

3 The hotel manager is angry with Amy because she can be im_____ to guests.

4 I'm trying to phone Dan. I think that the number I've got is in_____ because it won't connect.

5 Hannah designs her own clothes. They're always more un_____ than clothes you buy in the shops.

6 It's im_____ to concentrate in this office because you all talk too much.

7 Complete the sentences with these words and the correct prefix.

> correct ~~expensive~~ friendly patient
> tidy usual

1 I like going to markets because you can buy *inexpensive* jewellery and clothes.

2 I'm too _____ to wait for a taxi. It's quicker to walk home.

3 Alice smiled at the customers, but they were _____ and didn't want to talk to her.

4 The receptionist gave me the _____ key for my room and I couldn't open the door.

5 The shop is _____ because the customers look at things and then put them back in the wrong place.

6 It was _____ that Paul arrived late for work. He's often the first person there.

8 Complete the text with the best answer, A, B, C or D, for each space.

Dream job

I've always wanted to be a vet. I love animals and I don't mind working 1) _____ my own. Vets work long hours and often have to 2) _____ calm under pressure. Some big animals can be very difficult to work with and others are just 3) _____ and don't like people. I would always 4) _____ my best to help an animal that was sick. A vet's job is quite 5) _____ because they often have to work during the night and sleep during the day, but that isn't a problem for me. I don't want to 6) _____ a business as a vet. I'm not interested in 7) _____ money. I just want to help animals and offer 8) _____ treatment for sick animals.

1 A in   **B** on
   C for   D at
2 A spend   B be
   C stay   D stop
3 A unfriendly   B impolite
   C untidy   D unusual
4 A make   B have
   C show   D do
5 A incomplete   B impossible
   C incorrect   D unusual
6 A run   B make
   C work   D do
7 A enjoying   B making
   C doing   D working
8 A unusual   B expensive
   C inexpensive   D unfriendly

GRAMMAR

to + infinitive/-ing form

1 Complete the sentences with the full infinitive of these verbs.

> apply   ~~come~~   design   run
> speak   teach

1 Kate's promised _____to come_____ to the office this afternoon.
2 I've started _____ my own clothes.
3 It isn't easy _____ your own business at the moment.
4 Charlie and Hanna are learning _____ Russian.
5 Have you decided _____ for the job?
6 One day I want _____ in a primary school.

2 Complete the email. Use the *-ing* form of the verbs in brackets.

---

mailbox   Today | Mail | Calendar | Contacts

Reply | Reply All | Forward | Delete
From: **Naomi**   Subject: **Hi!**

Hi Dan
Have you finished 1) _____revising_____ (revise) for your last two exams? I can't imagine
2) _____ (have) two in one day! When you finish you can enjoy 3) _____ (do) nothing for a while.
Here's a photo of me with my young cousin, Luke. He's doing a summer camp and I'm helping. I'm interested in 4) _____ (work) with children one day so it's good experience.
Mum says I'm good at 5) _____ (entertain) them because I make them laugh.
I'm looking forward to 6) _____ (see) you in July. What date are you coming?
Write soon
Naomi

---

3 Choose the correct words.

1 I can't stand *working*/*to work* on my own. It's boring.
2 Will isn't interested in *making*/*to make* money.
3 Phoebe wants *selling*/*to sell* her own clothes.
4 What do you hope *doing*/*to do* in the future?
5 Harry doesn't mind *staying*/*to stay* late.
6 It isn't possible *finishing*/*to finish* this today.
7 Are you looking forward to *travel*/*travelling* around Europe?
8 I don't enjoy *working*/*to work* under pressure.

4 Complete the sentences. Use the correct form of the verbs in brackets. Sometimes more than one answer is possible.

1 It's important _____to be_____ (be) happy in your job.
2 Alice is good at _____ (bake). She should have a café.
3 They prefer _____ (work) for their dad.
4 Oliver has asked _____ (leave) early.
5 I love _____ (help) on my grandparents' farm.
6 They've arranged _____ (stay) for the summer.
7 We don't mind _____ (be) on our own.
8 The students start _____ (pick up) new skills quickly.

5 Complete the article with these verbs.

> making   meeting   selling   to get
> to help   to run   to speak   ~~working~~

How do you spend your summer? We're interested in hearing your stories. This week *Nick* tells us how he made the most of his holiday.

My parents have a small ice cream shop and last summer I started 1) _working_ in it. I really enjoyed 2) _____ customers and I was good at 3) _____ things to them. I also learned 4) _____ English well because a lot of the customers were American tourists. I think it's important 5) _____ some work experience before you leave school. One day I hope 6) _____ my own business and Dad's agreed 7) _____ me. I'm really interested in 8) _____ models of boats and I think I could sell them. In the photo you can see the latest boat I've made. Let me know what you think of it!

Indirect questions

6 Put the words in the correct order to make questions.

1 Can I ask you why / job / the / you /enjoy / ?
  Can I ask you why _____ *you enjoy the job?*
2 Do you know when / the / starts / job / ?
  Do you know when _____
3 Do you know if / will / team / be / in / you / a / ?
  Do you know if _____
4 Can you tell us where / you / work / will / ?
  Can you tell us where _____
5 Can I ask how long / here / you / worked / have / ?
  Can I ask how long _____
6 Could you tell us why / do / you / to / wanted / it / ?
  Could you tell us why _____

7 Put the words in brackets in the correct place in the questions.

1 Do you know the job is difficult? (if)
  Do you know if the job is difficult?
2 Can I ask you became a doctor? (why)
3 Can you tell us you trained? (where)
4 Can you tell us you stayed? (how long)
5 Could you tell me you got the job? (how)
6 Can you tell me I have to do today? (what)

8 Complete the interview with Sophie, a teenage dress designer. Use the questions in brackets to make indirect questions.

Fashion World

FW: Hi Sophie. I love your dress. Can I ask you 1) _if you made it?_ (Did you make it?).

Sophie: Yes, I made it for a friend's party.

FW: Can you tell us 2) _____ (How long does it take to design a dress?)

Sophie: It depends. Sometimes I can design a dress in a day, but sometimes it takes weeks.

FW: Could I ask you 3) _____ (When did you start designing?)

Sophie: When I left school, I did a course in clothes design.

FW: I see, and do you know 4) _____ (Are there many professional teenage designers?)

Sophie: Yes, there are. Some of them are very good.

FW: Do you know 5) _____ (What do you want to do in the future?)

Sophie: Yes, I'd love to run my own business.

FW: That's a great idea. Can I ask you 6) _____ (Have you made a dress for a famous person?)

Sophie: No, I haven't, but I'd like to one day.

FW: Well, good luck, Sophie.

Revision Units 9 – 10

VOCABULARY

1 Write the letters in the correct order to make hobby words. Complete the mystery sentence.

1 LEUG | G | L | U | E |
             9   2

2 TAPSYR | | | | | | |
              6

3 NERCES | | | | | | |
           16   4   8

4 TAERYTB | | | | | | |
          14   11

5 MOZO SELN | | | | | | | |
          3   10   5   12   15   13

6 CERPIE | | | | | |
          1

7 SSROCSSI | | | | | | | | |
          7   17

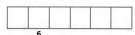

| | | | V | | | K | | | |
| 1 | 2 | 3 | 4 | 5 | 6 | 7 | 8 | 9 |

| | D | | | | | | D |
| 5 | 10 | 11 | 12 | 13 | 14 | 15 |

| | | K | | | |
| 16 | 17 | 3 | 1 | 8 | 9 |

2 Choose the correct words.

1 Jack and Dan don't like *keeping fit/online gaming* because they prefer doing sport outside.

2 We haven't got any homework tonight! Let's *chill out/ join in* at the beach.

3 That's a really nice necklace. I didn't know that you liked making *models/jewellery*.

4 There's a festival in the park. Why don't you go and *join in/hang out with* the fun?

5 *Cooking/Doing drama* is great, especially when you can eat the results.

6 Grace is saving for a new camera. She's *mad about/ hanging out with* taking photos.

3 Complete the phrases. There are two words you do not need.

> business   ~~challenge~~   creative   do
> money   on   skills   speak   stay   team

1 enjoy a *challenge*

2 pick up new _____ quickly

3 _____ calm under pressure

4 _____ my mind

5 always _____ your best

6 work _____ their own

7 run a _____

8 make _____

4 Complete the text with the best answer, A, B or C, for each space.

> My dad 1) _____ a sailing business and in the summer I enjoy helping him. I try to 2) _____ my best, but sometimes I don't know what I'm doing. He's great because he's never 3) _____ with me. He explains things slowly and always encourages me. He says I 4) _____ up new skills quickly. We have lots of customers in the summer, but Dad always stays 5) _____ under pressure. The only problem is the office. It's so 6) _____ because there are papers and books all over the floor. I try to organise it for him and keep it clean, but it's 7) _____!

1 A makes   **B** runs   C does

2 A do   B work   C speak

3 A unfriendly   B incorrect   C impatient

4 A put   B pull   C pick

5 A calm   B quiet   C silent

6 A incomplete   B untidy   C unusual

7 A impossible   B unfriendly   C inexpensive

GRAMMAR

1 Complete the reported sentences.

1 'I'll make a cake,' he said.
   He said that _he would make a cake_ .

2 'We can't find any batteries,' they said.
   They said that _____ .

3 'The work in the hotel is interesting,' she said.
   She said that _____ .

4 'I'm mad about taking photos,' Nick said.
   Nick said that he _____ .

5 'My camera isn't working,' Lucy told me.
   Lucy told me that _____ .

6 'Your dinner is ready,' their dad said.
   Their dad told them _____ .

7 'We enjoy doing drama after school,' the girls said.
   The girls said that _____ .

8 'I don't like difficult recipes,' Max said.
   Max said that _____ .

2 Complete the blog with the correct form of *used to* and the verbs in brackets.

💬 View previous comments   Cancel   Share   Post

When you were young 1) _did you use to have_
(you / have) a favourite hobby? I was mad about
collecting things. I 2) _____ (love)
big, old keys and every time I found one I
3) _____ (put) it in a very old box
which I locked with a special key.
I 4) _____ (not do) anything with the
keys. I just 5) _____ (like) looking at
them. I tried to imagine who the key belonged to.
6) _____ (they / live) in a huge house
with a big door? What happened to them?
I 7) _____ (believe) that every key
had its own story.
What about you? Do you have an unusual hobby?
I'd love to hear about it.

Write a comment   Support

3 Complete the sentences with the infinitive or the *-ing* form of these verbs.

be	help	make	run	speak	stay
		take	~~work~~		

1 Do you enjoy _working_ on your own?
2 She's good at _____ her own clothes.
3 They hope _____ a computer business one day.
4 Are you interested in _____ photos of animals?
5 Olivia has agreed _____ us in the café this afternoon.
6 I think it's important _____ a good team player.
7 It isn't easy for James _____ his mind.
8 Dan doesn't mind _____ late because he loves his job.

4 Complete the indirect questions.

1 When did you start making websites?
   Can you tell us when _you started_ making websites?

2 Where did you study website design?
   Can I ask you _____ website design?

3 Is it easy to find work?
   Do you know if _____ to find work?

4 What sort of computer have you got?
   Could you tell me what sort of computer _____ ?

5 How long does it take to make a website?
   Can I ask _____ to make a website?

6 Are there many teenage web designers?
   Do you know if _____ many teenage web designers?

VOCABULARY

1 Match two squares to make a word. Find nine natural world words and write them under the correct heading.

~~pa~~	so	sa
nd	st	cl
mi	cl	mo
~~th~~	il	oud
iff	st	ck
ar	on	ro

Sky/weather	Ground
	path

2 Complete the words with *a*, *e*, *i*, *o* or *u*.

1 cl _o_ _u_ d
2 s___nsh___n___
3 w___v___s
4 w___t___rf___ll
5 s_____l
6 m_____n
7 ___v___l___nch___
8 p___th

3 Write the letters in the correct order to make natural world words and complete the sentences.

1 We couldn't see where we were going because the ___*mist*___ (stmi) was bad.
2 The ski instructor told them to go home because there was danger of an _____ (vnehalaca).
3 When we saw the high _____ (vsawe) we decided to go surfing.
4 Max was worried when he saw his friends walking along the top of the _____ (fcfil).
5 Grace and her friend were relaxing in the sun when they saw a black _____ (dcolu) in the distance.
6 It's so hot at the beach today that it's impossible to walk on the _____ (ndas).

4 Complete the email with the correct word. The first letter has been given.

Subject: **Camping**

Hi Ben
This mountain campsite is fantastic. We arrived late last night, but it was still light because there was a full 1) m _oon_ _____. You could see hundreds of 2) s_____. It was so cool. This morning there isn't a 3) c_____ in the sky and it's very warm. I hope this 4) s_____ lasts, but I don't think it will. The owner of the campsite says it will be windy tomorrow and there could be a 5) s_____ because they get a lot at the end of the summer. This morning we're going for a walk. There's a 6) p_____ that goes up to a 7) w_____ where we hope to swim. The water will be freezing!
See you soon.
Anna

5 Complete the information in the holiday brochure with these words. There are two words you do not need.

cliff mist paths sand soil stars ~~sunshine~~ waterfall waves

Island Adventure Centre

Come on your own or come with friends. With around 325 days of 1) _sunshine_ every year you won't be bored at Island Adventure Centre! You can surf the 2) _____, play beach volleyball on the soft white 3) _____ or join us on an exciting midnight walk along one of the beautiful mountain 4) _____ that lead to the highest 5) _____ in Turkey. Our adventure centre is located on the top of a 6) _____ with amazing views of the mountains behind and the sea in front. In the evenings we also offer boat trips with music so you can dance all night and watch the 7) _____ in the sky at the same time.

6 Write these adjectives under the correct heading.

~~beautiful~~ blue dangerous deep high horrible interesting new old scary

Opinion	Fact
beautiful	

7 Match the sentence beginnings (1–7) with the endings (A–G).

1 They live in a big, _C_
2 Marie's making a wonderful, ___
3 She's wearing a strange, ___
4 They're swimming in a dangerous, ___
5 We're looking at the small, ___
6 I couldn't walk on the hot, ___
7 Harry followed the scary, ___

A blue coat.　　**E** deep lake.
B white stars.　**F** long path.
C old house.　　**G** chocolate cake.
D black sand.

8 Complete the blog with the best answer, A, B or C, for each space.

Natureblog.com

💬 View previous comments　Cancel　Share　Post

The power of the sea
We all love watching the 1) _____ waves at the beach and some of us surf in them, but on a recent geography trip I discovered how much damage they cause. When it's very windy, strong waves hit the 2) _____, and the power of the water breaks up the 3) _____ and stone which fall and create the beach below. Sometimes you get a 4) _____ beach, but in some areas the 5) _____ is black because the beach is near a volcano. Strong 6) _____ can then pull the beach back into the sea. Another problem is that plants are dying because the 7) _____ that they live in is carried away by the wind and waves.

Write a comment　　　Support

1 **A** big, amazing　**B** amazing and big
　Ⓒ amazing, big
2 **A** paths　　**B** cliffs
　C clouds
3 **A** rock　　**B** soil
　C sand
4 **A** beautiful, white　**B** beautiful and white
　C white, beautiful
5 **A** soil　　**B** sand
　C cliff
6 **A** rocks　　**B** waves
　C sunshine
7 **A** mist　　**B** soil
　C rock

GRAMMAR

Present simple passive and past simple passive

1 Choose the correct words.

1 The sand on the beach *is/are* cleaned every morning.
2 This fruit *isn't/aren't* used for cooking because it tastes disgusting.
3 The waterfall *is/are* often photographed at night.
4 The tickets for the trip *isn't/aren't* included in the price of the holiday.
5 Your help *isn't/aren't* needed at the moment.
6 The forest plants *is/are* used to make medicine.

2 Complete the sentence with *was*, *were*, *wasn't* or *weren't*.

1 They believe that the avalanche ____*was*____ caused by the change in temperature.
2 The mystery rock _____ discovered until ten years ago.
3 All the sandwiches _____ eaten on the long walk in the mountains.
4 Ben and Hannah _____ warned about the river, but still went swimming.
5 The moon _____ covered by the clouds so we couldn't see it.
6 The animals _____ given enough food and they were still hungry.

3 Find nine past participles.

c	e	t	f	o	u	n	d
c	r	e	a	t	e	d	t
b	b	d	l	t	e	t	a
u	o	i	a	k	n	m	e
e	u	e	c	e	t	a	e
b	g	e	k	p	e	d	a
c	h	a	e	t	n	e	e
c	t	k	t	a	e	c	k

4 Complete the sentences. Use the verbs in brackets and the passive form of the tenses given.

1 The tourists ____*are warned*____ (warn) to leave the beach when there's a red flag. (present simple)
2 The children _____ (not teach) in the villages where they live. (present simple)
3 This photo _____ (take) when we were in India. (past simple)
4 More help _____ (need) if we are going to change this situation. (present simple)
5 The rubbish bags _____ (collect) early each morning. (present simple)
6 Dangerous animals _____ (not use) in the documentary. (past simple)
7 The river _____ (clean) by volunteers every year. (present simple)
8 The small houses _____ (build) by their grandparents many years ago. (past simple)

5 Complete the newspaper report with these passive verbs.

> are covered   're told   's believed
> was heard   were given   were told
> ~~were warned~~

Last week tourists in the ski centre of Gretz 1) ____*were warned*____ about the possibility of an avalanche. Guests at the Mountain View Hotel 2) _____ to stay in their rooms. For two days nothing happened. One guest, Mr Hewlett, told us that his kids 3) _____ games and DVDs by the hotel, but they were still fed up. 'Imagine it', he said. 'We're in this beautiful place, the mountains 4) _____ in snow and we can't go out.' Then, on Friday morning, a sound 5) _____ high in the mountains. It was the avalanche. 'It was very scary', said Mr Hewlett. 'Now I know. If you 6) _____ to stay inside, you should stay inside.' It 7) _____ that ten people are still missing.

6 Read the email and complete the sentences. Use the correct form of the passive.

---

mailbox   Today | Mail | Calendar | Contacts

Reply | Reply All | Forward | Delete

From: **Aiden**   Subject: **Masca**

Dear Charlotte
I'm staying in an amazing village in Tenerife. They call it 'Masca' which means 'hidden'. Local people say that the village was a secret for many years. They didn't discover it until the 1960s. The people in the village built new houses and cafés. Now tourists visit it every day. Unfortunately young people don't need the new houses because they are leaving the village to work in the city. ☹ ☹
See you soon
Aiden

1 The village _____*is called*_____ Masca.
2 It _____ that the village was a secret for many years.
3 The village _____ until the 1960s.
4 A few years ago new houses and cafés _____ .
5 Now, it _____ by tourists every day.
6 The new houses _____ by young people because they're leaving the village.

---

could, should

7 Are the sentences suggestions (S), advice (A) or strong advice (SA)?

1 You should use sun cream when it's sunny.   *A*
2 We could visit the waterfall today. ....
3 You could try surfing as the waves are good. ....
4 You shouldn't wear those shoes on this dangerous path. ....
5 We could wait for better waves before we go surfing. ....
6 You should never go walking in the mountains if there's a storm. ....

8 Choose the correct words.

Anna: Hi, Mark. It's a lovely day. I think we 1) *should/shouldn't* go swimming in the lake this afternoon.

Mark: No, I don't want to. My dad says you 2) *couldn't/shouldn't* swim there because it isn't clean.

Anna: Oh, that's horrible. Well, we 3) *could/should* go for a walk and enjoy the sunshine.

Mark: OK, but it's very hot. If we go, 4) we *should/could* take lots of water.

Anna: Well, you 5) *could/should* bring the water and I'll get some food.

Mark: All right. Do you think I 6) *should/could* change?

Anna: Mark, of course you 7) *should/could*. You're in your hot school uniform!

12 Something new!

VOCABULARY

1 Complete the crossword with adjectives that describe experiences.

Across
1 difficult but interesting
3 enjoyable
6 good or useful
7 makes you want to do something

Down
2 very tiring
4 difficult and can cause problems
5 makes you feel calm and comfortable

2 Complete the words in the sentences with *a, e, i, o* or *u*.

1 It was a t _o_ _u_ gh competition so James was surprised when he won.
2 Learning to cook was l___f___-ch___ng___ng for me.
3 Amelia said it was ___mb___rr___ss___ng when she dropped her lunch on the floor.
4 After the exams we need a r___l___x___ng day at the beach.
5 The science trip was a p___s___t___v___ experience for the students.
6 Climbing the mountain in the rain was ___xh___st___ng.
7 The drama students found the actor's visit to the school very m___t___v___t___ng.
8 The sign language course is ch___ll___ng___ng at first, but most students enjoy it.

3 Match the questions (1–6) with the answers (A–F).

1 Was your party fun, Liam? _D_
2 It's very motivating when you get good exam results. ___
3 You look very tired, Jessica. ___
4 How was the volleyball competition? ___
5 I'd like to do something positive this summer. ___
6 I think this exercise is tough. ___

A Yes, it is. Now I'm looking forward to starting my new course in September.
B Yes, it is, but if we do it together it will be easier.
C It was really challenging, but we won in the end.
D Yes, but tidying up at the end of it was exhausting. It took ages!
E I am. I need a relaxing holiday in the sun.
F Why don't you help at the children's summer camp? It's good experience.

4 Choose the correct words.

A summer with a difference

In the summer I usually hang out with friends and have lots of 1) *tough/relaxing* days at the beach. However, this year I've decided to do something 2) *challenging/exhausting* in the holidays. I enjoy writing stories in my free time because it's 3) *life-changing/fun* so I've decided to do a creative writing course. Today was the first day. The first thing we had to do was stand up and talk about ourselves. I couldn't think what to say and my face went red! It was very 4) *embarrassing/motivating*! Then we wrote a poem which was really 5) *motivating/tough* because poems are difficult for me. But after we read them in class, the teacher said some very 6) *positive/embarrassing* things about mine. I was so happy.

5 Read the definitions and complete the phrasal verbs.

1	become something different	turn	*into*
2	start doing a new job or hobby	take	
3	stop doing something	give	
4	happen	take	
5	organise something	sort	
6	discover	find	
7	be involved in an event	take	
8	continue doing something	keep	

6 Choose the correct phrasal verbs.

1 We couldn't *find out/take part in* the price of the course so we didn't go.
2 Alice doesn't want to *keep on/give up* her English classes because they help her a lot.
3 I'm going to *take place/take part in* the school play because I love acting.
4 Can you *sort out/take up* the problem with this camera? I don't know what's wrong.
5 We've *given up/taken up* running because we want to get fit.
6 First the rain and now the snow. This picnic is *turning into/taking place* a disaster.

7 Choose the best answer, A, B or C.

1 I'm not going to .... my drama class because I enjoy doing the shows.
   A give up   **B** keep on   **C** take up
   (A circled)
2 It was .... for Jack when he sent his email to the wrong person.
   A life-changing   **B** exhausting
   C embarrassing
3 A new first-aid course will .... at the school this weekend.
   A take part in **B** take place **C** find out
4 I wanted to .... the piano, but I couldn't find a teacher.
   A take up   **B** turn into   **C** keep on
5 Meeting the film director was .... for Kate because he helped her become an actor.
   A relaxing   **B** challenging
   C life-changing
6 He used to be lazy, but he's .... the best student in the class.
   A turned into **B** sorted out **C** given up

8 Complete the information with these adjectives and phrasal verbs.

> exhausting   find out   gave up
> is taking place   ~~keep on~~   positive
> take part in   tough

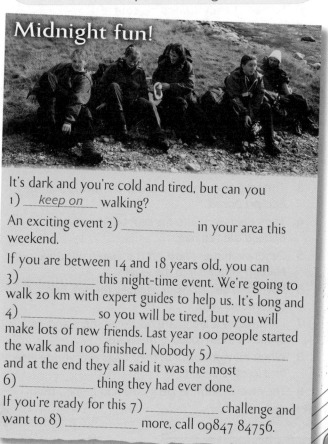

Midnight fun!

It's dark and you're cold and tired, but can you 1) *keep on* walking?

An exciting event 2) .... in your area this weekend.

If you are between 14 and 18 years old, you can 3) .... this night-time event. We're going to walk 20 km with expert guides to help us. It's long and 4) .... so you will be tired, but you will make lots of new friends. Last year 100 people started the walk and 100 finished. Nobody 5) .... and at the end they all said it was the most 6) .... thing they had ever done.

If you're ready for this 7) .... challenge and want to 8) .... more, call 09847 84756.

GRAMMAR

Past perfect simple and past simple

1 Complete the sentences. Use the past perfect form of the verbs in brackets.

1 I _'d/had spoken_ (speak) to Sophie.
2 We ＿＿＿＿＿＿＿＿ (not see) the film.
3 It ＿＿＿＿＿＿＿ (not snow) for five years.
4 Did you think that Theo ＿＿＿＿＿＿＿ (finish)?
5 He ＿＿＿＿＿＿＿ (try) learning the guitar before.
6 James ＿＿＿＿＿＿ (learn) something new.

2 Match the sentence beginnings (1–6) with the endings (A–F).

1 When I met Mark, _D_
2 The show began ＿＿＿
3 After the party had finished, ＿＿＿
4 We had just left a message for Anna ＿＿＿
5 I had waited an hour for the bus ＿＿＿
6 He didn't do the class ＿＿＿

A they tidied up the house.
B when it finally came.
C because he had left his guitar at home.
D he had already started his course.
E when she arrived.
F before the girls had found their seats.

3 Choose the action that happens first in each sentence.

1 Alex and his friends decided *to go to the beach* after they _had finished studying_.
2 It *had been* warm all day, but it was very windy when *they arrived.*
3 They *sat* on the sand and ate the picnic that they *had prepared.*
4 Then they *went into the sea*, but they *hadn't noticed* the red flag.
5 Other swimmers *had left* the water, but Alex and Nathan *jumped* into the waves.
6 It *was difficult to swim* because the sea *had become* so wild.
7 Fortunately a life guard *had seen* them and he *called* to them to leave the water.
8 When they *got back* to their bags everybody else *had left* the beach.
9 They *were glad* the life guard *had helped* them.

4 Choose the correct words.

1 Sam's friends arrived before he _had eaten_/ate his breakfast.
2 The course had already started when Hannah *had decided/decided* to do it.
3 Last week I found a camera that somebody *had left/left* on the beach.
4 After Nick *had had/had* a few lessons, he began to cook for his friends.
5 A boy in Brazil *had called/called* Sonia because he had found her message in a bottle.
6 I *hadn't called/didn't call* you last night because I had had an exhausting day.
7 We were surprised when we heard that we *had won/won* the competition.
8 They *hadn't spent/didn't spend* all their money when they finished shopping.

5 Complete the article. Use the correct form of the verbs in brackets.

AN ARTISTIC SUMMER

Last summer I stayed with an aunt who 1) _had invited_ (invite) me to spend the school holidays with her. She 2) ＿＿＿＿＿＿＿＿ (just / open) a summer school for young artists and asked me to help. I'd always got on well with her and 3) ＿＿＿＿＿＿＿ (want) to go. The school had just started when I 4) ＿＿＿＿＿＿ (arrive). Most of the students were between 14 and 18 and some of them 5) ＿＿＿＿＿＿＿ (win) prizes for their art at school. Each day I 6) ＿＿＿＿＿＿ (help) my aunt with the various activities that she had planned. One day I took a group of students to a park where some artists 7) ＿＿＿＿＿＿ (arrange) an exhibition of huge sculptures. They were so cool. Before I stayed with my aunt I 8) ＿＿＿＿＿＿ (not think) much about art. Now I can't wait to be one of her students.

6 Complete the magazine interview with the best answer, A, B or C, for each space.

One lucky teenager from Turkey has just had a very exciting summer. Three months ago, Ali Gezmen won a competition for a place at a circus summer camp. So what was it like? At *Circus World* we went to find out.

CW: What did you think when you found out that you 1) _____ a place at the circus summer camp?

AG: I was really surprised. I 2) _____ that a lot of people had entered the competition. I didn't think I'd win.

CW: Had you had any experience of circus skills before you 3) _____ the summer camp?

AG: I 4) _____ a short course in juggling, but I wasn't very good.

CW: When did you decide to enter the competition?

AG: Well, I'd seen the circus a few times and then one day I 5) _____ about the summer camp on the radio.

CW: What were the other students like, Ali?

AG: They were really nice. Some of them 6) _____ a long way for the camp.

CW: Did you miss your friends and family at home?

AG: Yes, I did, but after I 7) _____ a few new friends I was fine.

CW: What was the best thing about the circus summer camp?

AG: I learned something new. I 8) _____ unicycling before I did the summer camp and now I'm mad about it.

CW: Thanks Ali.

1 **A** 've won   **B** won   **C** 'd won
2 **A** knew   **B** know   **C** 've known
3 **A** joined   **B** 'd joined **C** 've joined
4 **A** 've done   **B** 'd done   **C** do
5 **A** 'd heard   **B** 've heard **C** heard
6 **A** had travelled
   B have travelled
   C has travelled
7 **A** 'd made   **B** make   **C** 've made
8 **A** haven't tried **B** hadn't tried **C** didn't try

have/get something done

7 Write the words in the correct order to make sentences.

1 has / her / She / hair / cut / Paul / by / .
   She has her hair cut by Paul.

2 this afternoon / I / to / my / get / bike / want / repaired / .

3 do / eyes / you / your / Where / tested / have / ?

4 my / I'm / invitations / printed / having / .

5 not / I'm / getting / coloured / my / hair / .

6 checked / We / the / must / get / computer / .

8 Complete the sentences. Use the present simple or present continuous of *have/get* and the correct form of the verb in brackets.

1 I _have/get_ my teeth _checked_ every year. (check)

2 They often _____ their skateboards _____ in the shop. (repair)

3 Emma _____ her photo _____ at the moment. (take)

4 Daniel always _____ his hair _____ by his dad. (cut)

5 Where _____ your costumes _____ ? (you / make)

6 We _____ the classrooms _____ this year. (not paint)

Revision Units 11 – 12

VOCABULARY

1 Complete the postcard with natural world words. The first letter has been given.

Hi Anna
I'm having a brilliant time in Cuba. After the bad 1) _storm_ last night with rain and wind, today the weather is great with lots of 2) s_____.
There isn't a 3) c_____ in the sky.
The hotel is on the top of a
4) c_____ and the views are amazing. Behind the hotel there's a
5) p_____ that you can walk down to the beach. The sea is an incredible colour and the 6) s_____ is soft and white. This afternoon we hope to go surfing because there are some great
7) w_____.
See you soon
Max

2 Complete the sentences with the adjectives in brackets in the correct order.

1 They were going back to their tent when they saw some ____big black____ clouds. (black/big)

2 We put our towels down on the _____ sand. (smooth/white)

3 I don't want to watch another _____ film. (old/boring)

4 They ate all of that _____ cake. (lovely/strawberry)

5 The children were drawing _____ stars on the wall. (yellow/small)

6 In the moon they could see the face of a(n) _____ man. (old/funny)

3 Complete the diary entry with these adjectives.

challenging   embarrassing   exhausting
~~fun~~   positive   relaxing

My first camping trip in the mountains and I'm really enjoying it. I never knew camping could be 1) ___fun___! The journey here took four hours, but it was 2) _____ because we chatted and listened to music. Unfortunately poor Charlie was sick and the coach had to stop at the side of the road. It was so 3) _____ for him! When we arrived we had an 4) _____ two-hour walk up the mountain to the campsite. Everybody was tired and then we had to put up the tents. Some of us didn't know how to do it. The teachers said that this trip would be 5) _____ for us because we come from the city. Some of us have never camped before. However, with the teachers' help, I think this will be a really 6) _____ week for us all.

4 Rewrite the sentences. Use a phrasal verb to replace the underlined words.

1 It was a long exhausting walk, but nobody <u>stopped</u>.
   It was a long exhausting walk, but nobody gave up.

2 A big party will <u>happen</u> on the last night of the camping trip.
   _____

3 I don't want this holiday to <u>become</u> a disaster.
   _____

4 Let's <u>discover</u> how much the trip costs.
   _____

5 Alice is going to <u>organise</u> the tickets and the travel arrangements.
   _____

6 Do you want to <u>continue</u> with your piano lessons?
   _____

GRAMMAR

1 Complete the passive sentences. Use *by* where necessary.

1 They take photos on the last day of school.
   Photos *are taken* on the last day of school.

2 The students performed a musical.
   A musical _____ the students.

3 They give the best student a prize.
   A prize _____ to the best student.

4 The students don't take the books home.
   The books _____ home.

5 They don't wear uniforms on the last day.
   Uniforms _____ on the last day.

6 They make plans for the summer.
   Plans _____ for the summer

7 The teachers prepare a party.
   A party _____ the teachers.

8 One of the students filmed a video.
   A video _____ one of the students.

2 Complete the conversation. Use the past perfect or past simple form of the verbs in brackets.

Hannah: Hi, Sam, you look fed up.

Sam: I am. I 1) _____ *went* _____ (go) into town this morning with Gemma because we 2) _____ (arrange) to do a babysitting course. Gemma had seen an advert for it online and we 3) _____ (like) the idea.

Hannah: So what happened?

Sam: When we got there the course 4) _____ (start). The teacher said that the course was full and we couldn't join.

Hannah: 5) _____ (you / already / book) a place?

Sam: Yes, we had and we 6) _____ (call) to confirm the place after we'd sent the money.

Hannah: So what happened?

Sam: There was a mistake on their computer. They 7) _____ (not book) Gemma and me on a babysitting course. They 8) _____ (book) us on a course in flower arranging and we didn't want to do that!

3 Write the words in the correct order to make sentences.

1 could / your / old / You / clothes / recycle / .
   You could recycle your old clothes.

2 we / shop / should / Maybe / to / another / go / ?

3 You / his / use / phone / shouldn't / .

4 try / Should / different / we / a / path / ?

5 shouldn't / You / there / bag / leave / your / .

6 We / stars / the / watch / tonight / could / .

4 Write sentences. Use *have/get* and the tenses in brackets.

1 Jessica / her dress / make / for the school party.
   (present continuous)
   Jessica is getting/having her dress made for the school party.

2 We / our eyes / check / every year.
   (present simple)

3 The students / their exams / mark / now
   (present continuous)

4 you / the room / decorate / for the event?
   (present continuous)

5 I / never / my photo / take / in the morning.
   (present simple)

6 They / the food and drinks / deliver / to the festival. (present simple)

Pearson Education Limited
Edinburgh Gate
Harlow
Essex CM20 2JE
England
and Associated Companies throughout the world.

www.pearsonelt.com

First published 2014
Seventh impression 2019

ISBN: 978-1-4479-1393-1

Set in 10pt Mixa ge ITC Std
Printed by Malaysia, CTP-PJB

Acknowledgements
*The publishers and author would like to thank the following people for
their feedback and comments during the development of the material:*

Elif Berk, Turkey; Alan Del Castillo Castellanos, Mexico; Dilek Kokler,
Turkey; Trevor Lewis, The Netherlands; Nancy Ramirez, Mexico;
Jacqueline Van Mil-Walker, The Netherlands

The publisher would like to thank the following for their kind
permission to reproduce their photographs:

(Key: b-bottom; c-centre; l-left; r-right; t-top)

Alamy Images: Alexander Caminada 55tl, Bernadette Delaney 35br,
CountrySideCollection – Homer Sykes 59br, Cultura RM 41bl, Dennis
MacDonald 35cl, Directphoto.org 17b, incamerastock 38cl, Jeff
Greenberg 61bl, Judith Collins 30tl, Keith Morris 51tl, Lebrecht Music
and Arts Photo Library 10r, PhotoAlto 35tr, Radius Images 63bl, Steve
Gottlieb 40br, tbkmedia.de 30tr; **Corbis:** Daniel Munoz / Reuters 5b,
Ocean 9r; **DK Images:** Alex Robinson 60br, Andy Crawford 44tl, Gary
Ombler 44tr, Linda Burgess 44bl, Nikid Design Ltd 44cr, Trish Gant
35cr; **Fotolia.com:** Akbudak Rimma 35bl, Alehdats 44cl, Corinaldo
38br, Faabi 26bl, Okinawakasawa 44br, Raywoo 30bl; **Getty Images:**
Dori OConnell 50br, Matthew Lloyd 33br; **Pearson Education Ltd:**
Gareth Boden 12c, 19b, Handan Erek 12tl, Jon Barlow 12tr, 12b, 57r;
Rex Features: APA 38tl; **Shutterstock.com:** 26br, Dmitry Berkut 38cr,
Lenetstan 36r, Markus Mainka 38tr, Mitch Gunn 27br, Peresanz 46br,
Stuart Monk 43bl, viki2win 35tl, Whitelook 38bl; **SuperStock:** Age
fotostock 57l, Fotosearch 25b, Marka 62l

Cover images: *Front:* **Fotolia.com:** Alexander Yakovlev

All other images © Pearson Education

Every effort has been made to trace the copyright holders and we
apologise in advance for any unintentional omissions. We would be
pleased to insert the appropriate acknowledgement in any subsequent
edition of this publication.